Attitude Research
Enters The 80's

Attitude Research Enters The 80's

Richard W. Olshavsky, Editor
Indiana University

AMERICAN MARKETING ASSOCIATION

Proceedings Series

222 South Riverside Plaza - Chicago, Illinois 60606 - (312) 648-0536

Cover Design by Mary Jo Krysinski

Library of Congress Cataloging in Publication Data

Attitude Research Conference, 11th, Carlsbad, Calif.,
    1980.
    Attitude research enters the '80s.

    1. Motivation research (Marketing)--Congresses.
2. Marketing research--Congresses. I. Olshavsky,
Richard W., 1941-   II. American Marketing Association.
III. Title.
HF5415.3.A877 1980   658.8'342   80-20621
ISBN 0-87757-145-7

                                    174/1000/980

TABLE OF CONTENTS

FOREWORD

Attitude Research Enters the '80s is the proceedings of
the American Marketing Association's 1980 Attitude Research
Conference. The Conference was held at La Costa Hotel & Spa,
Carlsbad, California, March 2-5, 1980.

The organization of these proceedings follows the conference program as set forth by Alden G. Clayton, the 1980
Program Chairman.

This proceedings was prepared from camera-ready copy
supplied by the authors.

IDEAS ON INTEGRATING ATTITUDE THEORY WITH INFORMATION PROCESSING THEORY

Jerry C. Olson, Pennsylvania State University, University Park[1]

ABSTRACT

This paper presents several ideas concerning how to integrate attitude theory with broader, more abstract theories of information processing. The novel perspectives to attitude research and to existing attitude data provided by such an approach are emphasized. The utility of the advocated information processing perspective is demonstrated by generating new questions regarding attitude theory and by identifying implications of the proposed approach for future attitude research. The paper is entirely conceptual; data are not presented.

INTRODUCTION

An old saying, now almost a cliche, states: "There's nothing so practical as a good theory." While true enough, we must not overlook the other side of that coin--namely: "There's nothing more dangerous than a bad theory." Where does attitude theory belong? I believe that current attitude <u>theory</u> is in reasonably good shape, although there are frequent measurement problems at the empirical level.[2] Thus, the following remarks are intended to help place current attitude theory into the broader conceptual framework provided by information processing theory. Integrating attitude theory with the information processing perspective is not an original idea. Others have tried to do so (cf., Calder 1975; 1978; Cohen 1979; Holbrook 1978; Lutz 1977; Olson and Mitchell 1975; Olson and Dover 1978). All seemed to believe that an information processing perspective can make attitude theory more coherent, more powerful, and more useful predictively. This paper can be seen as an additional step toward integrating attitude and information processing theories.

[1]Associate Professor of Marketing, Pennsylvania State University, University Park, PA 16802. Preparation of this paper was partially supported by the Science and Education Administration of the U.S. Department of Agriculture under Grant No. 5901-0410-8-0151-0 from the Competitive Research Grants Office.

[2]Theoretical constructs are often poorly operationalized. Consequently, purported tests of a theory do not do so, and the obtained data are not relevant to the validity of the theory.

1

WHAT IS ATTITUDE THEORY?

What is attitude theory? Actually, of course, there are
many theories regarding attitude (cf., Calder and Shur in press;
McGuire 1968). Although superficially different, most of these
conceptualizations are in fact rather similar. Before reviewing
these perspectives, however, we must first consider what an
attitude is.

Attitude Construct

Over the last 50 to 60 years, psychologists have proposed
many definitions of attitude (cf., Fishbein and Ajzen 1975).
These include Allport's (1935) classic statement that attitude
is an enduring disposition to behave consistently toward an
object. Others have considered attitude as an evaluative or
affective or emotional (internal) response toward an object
(Thurstone 1931; Fishbein 1963; 1967). The tripartite definition of attitude as consisting of cognitive, affective, and
conative components has been and still is popular (Ostrom 1969;
Bagozzi, Tybout, Craig and Sternthal 1979).

All of these definitions share one characteristic--namely,
attitude is an internal response that is (at least partially)
affective or evaluative in nature. Probably a majority of mar-
keting/consumer researchers would agree that "the characteristic
that distinguishes attitude from other concepts is its evaluative
or affective nature (Fishbein and Ajzen 1975, p. 11)." Thus,
in this paper, the term attitude refers to the internal, uni-
dimensional affect of evaluative feeling associated with a concept or object.

Attitude Theory

More clearly than most, Fishbein's (1963; 1967) theory
addresses the basic issues of what causes this evaluative/
affective attitude response and how is it related to other constructs. As we all know, his perspective has had the major impact on the attitude research conducted by marketing researchers.
Briefly, Fishbein considers attitude to be a function of a set
of salient beliefs regarding an object. Specifically, one's
attitude toward an object (A_o) or a behavioral act (A_{act}) is a
function of the evaluations (e_i) that are associated with the
relevant or salient beliefs about the object, each weighted
by the strength of belief (b_i) that the object is associated
with that belief attribute (i). Usually the strengths and
evaluations of multiple salient beliefs are multiplied and then
summed to yield an indicator of global attitude toward the
object ($\Sigma\ b_i e_i$). Thus, Fishbein's identity model $\Sigma\ b_i e_i = A_o$
captures the causal basis for attitude. Attitude is a function
of the cognitive knowledge (beliefs) one possesses about an

object. In an extension of this model, Fishbein further proposed that attitudes are a primary causal influence on intentions to behave (BI), which in turn are a major determinant of overt behavior (see Fishbein and Ajzen 1975).

There are disagreements as to the causal basis for attitude (for a recent alternative view, see Zajonc 1980): however, the "beliefs-cause-attitude-causes-intentions-causes-behavior" model has several advantages. For instance, the causal flow from beliefs to attitudes to intentions to behavior essentially incorporates the tripartite definition of attitude and explicitly specifies the causal interrelationships between the three components. Unfortunately, rigorous tests of these causal relationships are difficult and consequently they are rare (see Lutz 1975; 1977) and somewhat controversial (Dickson and Miniard 1978; Carnegie-Mellon University Marketing Seminar 1978). However, most researchers have found correlational support for the predicted associations. In fact, we **have** a large body of static, cross-sectional investigations **which have obtained positive correlations between purported measures of these constructs (see Wilkie and Pessemier 1973).**

Over the course of this extensive research effort, operational controversies have tended to dominate many researchers' interests. Often fairly trivial issues have assumed major proportions. Issues such as normalization of model components and aggregation vs. disaggregation of the model once captured the interests of many attitude researchers. Today such issues, although unresolved, seem much less important than they once did. For many, the net outcome of this extensive effort has been discouragement with, even hostility toward, the so-called multiattribute modeling approach to attitudes. Adding to these negative feelings about attitude theory and research is the wide variety of apparent empirical aberrations in the results. For instance, the cognitive structure index of attitude (e.g., $\Sigma \ b_i e_i$) has sometimes been only a weak predictor of a direct measure of global attitude ($\underline{A}_o$); correlations of .2–.4 are common. Attitude measures have occasionally been shown to be only moderately reliable, while attitudes often are poor predictors of behavior (see Fishbein and Ajzen 1975). Finally, situational factors seem to have an unnecessarily strong influence on the observed relationships. Apparently such problems have discouraged researchers since relatively little research has been published in the last two or three years. We seem to be sick of attitudes.

I prefer to believe, however, that researchers are sick of relatively trivial operational issues. The basic theoretical issues that underlie attitude research remain important, even central questions. For instance, how are attitudes (good-bad evaluations or likes and dislikes) formed? Are beliefs the only

3

causal influence on attitude? Can we change people's attitudes without changing their beliefs? How are our evaluations of objects related to our behavior toward them? These are important theoretical issues with clear practical significance.

Such issues have not decreased in significance, even though interest in attitude theory seems to have waned in recent years. Thus it seems reasonable to search for a theoretical perspective that can help us straighten out our thinking and our research practices regarding attitudes. A broader theoretical perspective may clarify some of the conceptual ambiguities. Perhaps such an approach can account for many of the apparent aberrations in our empirical data. I suggest that the theoretical ideas associated with human information processing may provide a useful framework within which that analysis can take place.

INFORMATION PROCESSING THEORY

Over the past 15 or so years, a powerful set of ideas has swept over psychology--namely, information processing theory. The information processing approach has had a major impact on experimental psychology and is beginning to **influence strongly** the more applied areas of social, developmental, and clinical psychology. Similarly, the effects of information processing theory have begun to affect consumer theory and research. By the early 1980's information processing will probably become the dominant influence on consumer research. Attitude theory and research may be one of the first consumer behavior areas to be incorporated into or integrated with an information processing perspective. This will necessarily be an evolutionary process that will take place over several years. Thus my remarks here are not the final word; rather they are offered as tentative ideas that are quite likely to be changed and modified by me and by others.

What is information processing theory? In fact, the word "theory" is probably a misnomer; "meta-theory" may be a more appropriate term. Information processing really involves a set of very broad, general, highly abstract ideas (see Lachman, Lachman, and Butterfield 1979). For the most part these ideas are not directly testable--that is, it is not possible to develop critical empirical tests of the validity of these ideas. Rather, the validity of these meta-theoretical ideas must be assumed, essentially taken on faith. However, because of their high level of abstraction, these ideas are extremely useful as they provide a conceptual framework within which normal theorizing and empirical research can take place.

Representation

What are the basic ideas regarding information processing

4

theory? I will briefly discuss four simple, but powerful ideas.
First, and probably most basic, is the idea that human mental
processes operate on the symbolic representations of stimuli.
Newell and Simon (cf., 1972), among others, have advocated this
notion, which is obviously influenced by the computer analogy.
Given this orientation, cognitive processes are seen as symbol
manipulating operations. Among the many implications of this
basic idea is the critical importance of cognitive representation. That is, how do we generate cognitive, symbolic representations of the world and what is the form and content of
those representations?

Processing Stages

The second basic idea is that the various mental operations,
the cognitive processes, are "linked together" as a processing
system. As one cognitive process finishes manipulating, trans-
forming or recoding (adding or subtracting meaning) the cognitive representations, other processing operations receive that
output and subject it to further processing. Figure 1 presents
my version of the common flow **chart** model of the basic cognitive
processes that are involved in information processing.

Memory Structure

A third meta-theoretical idea of importance is that the
very many representations each of us has acquired (about past
events in our lives and our knowledge of the world) are stored
in memory in an interrelated, organized way. It may be a convenient metaphor to consider that these representations are
stored in organized structures of knowledge. We could term
them belief structures, where the beliefs refer to the perceived
association between learned representations or cognitive concepts. Thus from an information processing perspective, a set
of beliefs is a cognitive structure of stored representations
and their associations.

Activation

Finally we have the fourth basic idea that stored representations, or structures of representations, can be recalled or
activated from memory merely by exposure to appropriate cue
stimuli. In this view of memory retrieval processes, exposure
to appropriate cues activate, or bring to consciousness, the
relevant representations. Thus, if someone asks you for your
home telephone number, somehow the cues present in the question
activate the stored representations of the number from memory,
in most cases almost immediately and automatically. Likewise,
it may be possible to activate entire well-learned structures
of knowledge, or schemata, from memory.

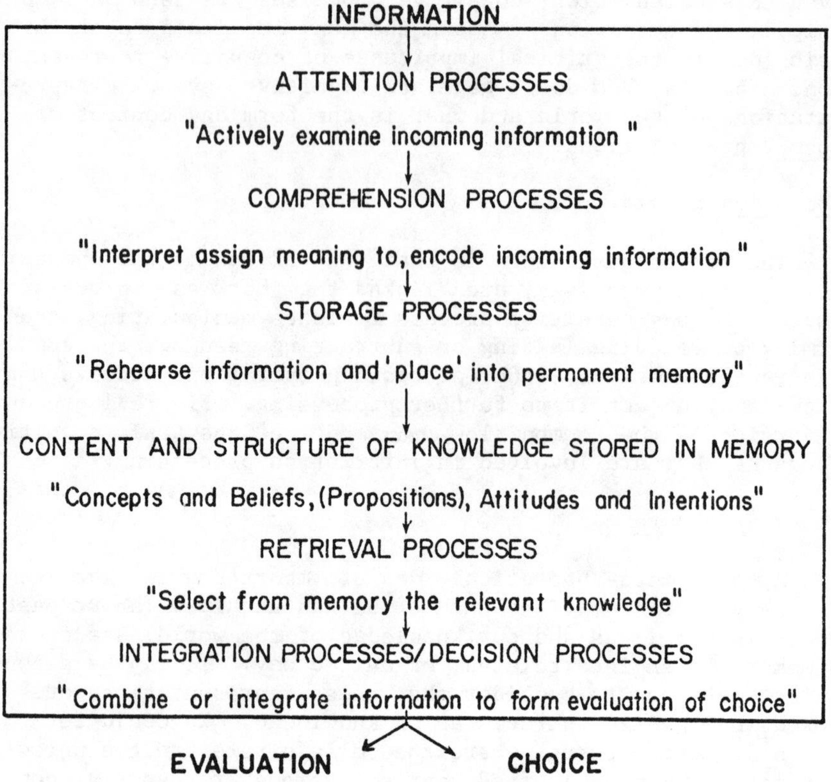

INFORMATION

ATTENTION PROCESSES

"Actively examine incoming information "

COMPREHENSION PROCESSES

"Interpret assign meaning to, encode incoming information "

STORAGE PROCESSES

"Rehearse information and 'place' into permanent memory"

CONTENT AND STRUCTURE OF KNOWLEDGE STORED IN MEMORY

"Concepts and Beliefs, (Propositions), Attitudes and Intentions"

RETRIEVAL PROCESSES

"Select from memory the relevant knowledge"

INTEGRATION PROCESSES/ DECISION PROCESSES

"Combine or integrate information to form evaluation of choice"

EVALUATION   CHOICE

FIGURE 1.   A Flow-Chart Representation of Major Cognitive
Processes and States Involved in Human Information
Processing.

In summary, these four basic assumptions constitute a large part of the meta-theoretical basis for the information processing approach. Once adopted by a researcher, these concepts can guide subsequent theorizing and empirical research. Now, these basic assumptions can be integrated with attitude theory to make the latter more consistent with the information processing perspective.

INTEGRATING ATTITUDE AND INFORMATION PROCESSING THEORY

Suppose I ask you how much you like Crest toothpaste. You might give me a verbal answer or perhaps a rating on a scale that I provide. Most researchers would consider your response as a relatively direct indicator of the internal, affective or evaluative feeling we have termed attitude. But how does this internal feeling develop? What factors cause the internal state and the overt response that we treat as an indicator. How are you able to answer my question, probably in a very short time, with relatively little cognitive effort?

We can begin to answer such questions by referring back to the basic assumption underlying an information processing approach.[3] What happens when I ask you to report your attitude toward Crest? Presumably the stimulus cue "Crest" activates the Crest representation and other stored cognitive representations associated with that concept. (Of course, there may be other cues in my question and in the immediate environment that may activate yet other representations, but we will ignore these problems for now.) Nearly everyone (in this culture at least) has probably acquired cognitive representations of concepts that are associated with the Crest representation. Some of these cognitive codes may represent product attributes such as "fluoride," or "mint taste." Other representations are also possible, however (cf., Calder 1978; Olson and Muderrisoglu 1979). For instance, you may know that Crest is manufactured and marketed by the Procter and Gamble Company. Or, you may possess a visual representation of the Crest package or the Crest logo. You may

---

[3]This perspective seems relevant since each of the issues raised above concerns cognitive processing. Certainly you must have processed (heard or read and comprehended) my question about Crest toothpaste in order to answer it. In all likelihood, much if not all of your evaluative feeling--your attitude--about Crest was originally derived from/through processing information about Crest. This information could have been generated from direct experience with the product, from advertisements, from friends, from one's dentist, and from many other sources. So, it seems reasonable to seek information processing answers to our questions.

have a visual representation of using Crest to brush your teeth this morning or a representation of Crest's taste. In sum, a wide variety of representations may be linked to the Crest representation and stored in an organized structure in memory.

The fact that most consumers probably possess a great many associations to any single representation raises another question. Which cognitive representations, of the many that may be associated with a concept such as Crest toothpaste, will be activated by my question? Here we can turn to the "spreading activation theory" proposed by Collins and Loftus (1975) as an extension of Quillian's (1967) earlier work on semantic memory. If we consider that stored representations are linked together through belief-like associations and are organized into network structures, it is but a short step to propose that the activation of one representation will spread to other representations throughout the network via the propositional belief linkages.

Surely, however, not every known association that you have linked to Crest toothpaste will be activated by my simple question. So, which of your many representations regarding Crest will be activated? Here we need the concept of "activation potential," which refers to the likelihood of a particular link between representations being activated. Activation potential will vary as a function of several factors, among them the recency of previous activation. We may assume that activation of a representation leaves a residual activation potential that gradually decays over time. Thus subsequent reactivation of a representation may be more likely due to the "extra" activation potential left over from the previous activation. Activation potential may also be influenced by the "degree" of association. Here, the concept of semantic relatedness is important. The more closely two representations are related in a meaningful, semantic sense, the more likely that activation of one will spread to and activate the other. As one example, consider the strong tendency to respond "chair" when given the cue "table." The term semantic relatedness seems to capture the key causal factor underlying this tendency.

Now, back to our original question. What happens when I ask you how much you like Crest toothpaste? Presumably, the cue "Crest," plus all the other cues that are available, will activate those representations you have acquired about Crest that currently have the highest activation potential. We can presume that each association or "belief" possesses an evaluative component. Following the logic of Fishbein's attitude theory (see Fishbein and Ajzen 1975), these individual evaluative aspects (e_i's) somehow combine (perhaps by an adding or an averaging process) to influence one's overall attitude toward Crest (A_o). Fishbein favors an additive model in which each e_i component is weighted by the strength of belief in the association (b_i); then all these weighted evaluations are summed to create global attitude: $\Sigma\ b_i e_i = A_o$. Other models are possible of course.

Given the information processing perspective advocated above, we could say then that one's attitude toward a concept (an object, idea, or act) is a function of the internal representations that are activated <u>at</u> <u>that</u> <u>particular</u> <u>time</u>, in that <u>situation</u>. In simple language, your attitude is determined by what you are thinking about. This is one major implication of the information processing perspective, and it raises a number of interesting questions about attitude research. The following section briefly discusses several of these issues.

IMPLICATIONS

Stability

How stable are one's attitudes? Certainly there is substantial variation between attitudes. Attitudes toward some concepts may be relatively stable while others are less stable. The proposed perspective can account for the lack of stability that may sometimes distress attitude researchers. In fact the advocated conceptual perspective predicts a fair degree of apparent instability. Consider the following. It is unlikely that thinking about most rather mundane consumer products and services over several different occasions will activate exactly the same set of cognitive associations each time. In fact, to the extent that one's cognitive structure is somewhat vague, diffuse, loosely organized, etc., we might expect substantial variation in the activated set of representations over multiple activation occasions. Also, other factors such as situational/ environmental cues or recent experiences will influence the activation process and the activated set of representations. Suppose I ask you to report your attitude toward Crest immediately after a visit to your dentist, and later after a consulting trip to Procter and Gamble headquarters in Cincinnati. I would expect to activate somewhat different representations in these two cases. Thus, I shouldn't be surprised to find that your stated attitude toward Crest may vary somewhat over these two measurement occasions.

In terms of the broader perspective provided by basic information processing theory, we might be less concerned by apparently low or moderate test-retest reliability coefficients (e.g., r's = .4 - .6). The attitude question could activate different representations at different times, leading to different attitudes. Thus, we would interpret our test-retest correlation coefficient differently and we might begin to

investigate the reasons for its fluctuation. A whole host of
questions would become interesting. How much variation can we
expect to find in the activated concepts for well known, familiar brands? What about unfamiliar brands? Are there differences for involving vs. uninvolving product categories? What
about the activated concepts of heavy vs. light vs. nonusers of
a product? And so on.

Attributes vs. Other Types of Representations

Another general issue of interest concerns the types of
representations that may be associated with a brand concept such
as Crest. Not all cognitive representations are likely to be
abstract product attributes like quality, convenience, style,
value-for-the money, etc., of which marketing researchers are
so fond. Many representations may be more concrete. For instance, cognitive representations associated with a brand could
be non-propositional visual images. Representations of other
sensory modalities such as auditory, tactile, and olfactory
could also be associated with a brand. According to the theory,
the evaluations associated with these "other" types of mental
representations should influence global attitude (A_o) in the
same way as the more traditional attribute representations.
But, do they? Could different processes occur for such representations? The issue of how affect is stored in a cognitive
structure consisting of varying types of representations is
fascinating and deserves attention in future research.

Context Specificity

Questions regarding the situational or context specificity
of attitudes have been raised frequently. Given our information processing perspective, it would not be surprising to find
that situational cues may occasionally have large effects on
the concepts that are activated, and thus on attitude. For
instance, different attributes may be activated when evaluating
a product for one purpose versus another (e.g., a gift vs. for
one's personal use). Thus, the advocated perspective can provide a more cognitive approach to research on situational effects.

IMPLICATIONS FOR ATTITUDE RESEARCH PRACTICE

Obviously, it is somewhat premature to propose specific
implications for attitude research. A great deal of basic
research needs to be conducted, within the broad framework
provided by the information processing paradigm, before it is
possible to recommend changes in attitude research practice.
At present, the advocated perspective can help us to see that

certain empirical results may not be really contrary to attitude theory. In fact, they may be expected. Also, the present perspective may make researchers more sensitive to the likely idiosyncracy of attitude structures. That is, each person has different representations and attitude structures. Although commercial attitude research may still require structured questionnaires that are identical for all subjects, at least we should recognize that these will necessarily be less accurate on an individual level than an approach specifically tailored to each subject's unique activated concepts.

SUMMARY

In this brief paper, I have tried to identify only a few of the perspectives and implications that an integration of attitude and information processing theory can provide. There are many other interesting issues not discussed here, including, for instance, attitude formation, attitude change, and the relations between attitudes and value systems. The point of the present paper is that the basic ideas of information processing "theory" can provide a useful, perhaps necessary perspective for addressing such issues. I expect this approach to attitude research to become more prominent over the next few years.

REFERENCES

Allport, Gordon W. (1935), "Attitudes," in Handbook of Social Psychology, C. Murchison, ed., Worchester, MA: Clark University Press.

Bagozzi, Richard P., Alice M. Tybout, C. Samuel Craig, and Brian Sternthal (1979), "The Construct Validity of the Tripartite Classification of Attitudes," Journal of Marketing Research, 16, 88-95.

Calder, Bobby J. (1975), "The Cognitive Foundations of Attitudes: Some Implications for Multi-Attribute Models," in Advances in Consumer Research, Vol. 2, M. J. Schlinger, ed., 241-247.

_____ (1978), "Cognitive Response, Imagery, and Scripts: What is the Cognitive Basis of Attitude?", in Advances in Consumer Research, Vol. 5, H. K. Hunt, ed., Ann Arbor, MI: Association for Consumer Research, 630-634.

_____ and Paul H. Shurr (in press), "Attitudinal Processes in Organizations," in Research in Organizational Behavior, Vol. 3, JAI Press.

Carnegie-Mellon University Marketing Seminar (1978), "Attitude
  Change or Attitude Formation? An Unanswered Question,"
  Journal of Consumer Research, 4, 271-276.

Cohen, Joel B. (1979), "Applying Expectancy-Value Models to
  Liking, Preference and Choice," a paper presented at the
  AMA's 10th Annual Attitude Research Conference, February
  25-29, Hilton Head, South Carolina.

Collins, Alan M. and Elizabeth F. Loftus (1975), "A Spreading
  Activation Theory of Semantic Processing," Psychological
  Review, 82, 407-428.

Dickson, Peter R. and Paul W Miniard (1978), "A Further Examination of Two Laboratory Tests of the Extended Fishbein
  Attitude Model," Journal of Consumer Research, 4, 261-266.

Fishbein, Martin (1963), "An Investigation of the Relationships
  Between Beliefs About an Object and the Attitude Toward
  That Object," Human Relations, 16, 233-240.

_____ (1967), "A Behavior Theory Approach to the Re-
  lations Between Beliefs About an Object and the Attitude
  Toward the Object," in Readings in Attitude Theory and
  Measurement, M. Fishbein, ed., New York: Wiley, 389-400.

_____ and Icek Ajzen (1975), Belief, Attitude, Intention
  and Behavior: An Introduction to Theory and Research,
  Reading, MA: Addison-Wesley.

Holbrook, Morris B. (1978), "Beyond Attitude Structure: Toward
  the Informational Determinants of Attitude," Journal of
  Marketing Research, 16, 545-556.

Lachman, Roy, Janet L. Lachman and Earl C. Butterfield (1979),
  Cognitive Psychology and Information Processing, Hillsdale,
  NJ: Lawrence Erlbaum.

Lutz, Richard J. (1975), "Changing Brand Attitudes Through
  Modification of Cognitive Structure," Journal of Consumer
  Research, 1, 49-59.

_____ (1977), "An Experimental Investigation of Causal
  Relations Among Cognitions, Affect, and Behavioral Intentions," Journal of Consumer Research, 3, 197-208.

McGuire, William J. (1968), "The Nature of Attitude and Attitude Change," in The Handbook of Social Psychology, Vol.
  3, G. Lindzey and E. Aronson, eds., Reading, MA: Addison-
  Wesley.

Newell, Alan and Herbert A. Simon (1972), <u>Human Problem Solving</u>, Englewood Cliffs, NJ: Prentice Hall.

Olson, Jerry C. and Philip A. Dover (1978), "Attitude Maturation: Changes in Related Belief Structures Over Time," in <u>Advances in Consumer Research</u>, Vol. 5, H. Keith Hunt, ed., Ann Arbor, MI: Association for Consumer Research, 333-342.

_____ and Andrew A. Mitchell (1975), "The Process of Attitude Acquisition: The Value of a Developmental Approach to Consumer Attitude Research," in <u>Advances in Consumer Research</u>, Vol. 2, M. J. Schlinger, ed., Chicago: Association for Consumer Research, 244-264.

_____ and Aydin Muderrisoglu (1979), "The Stability of Responses Obtained by Free Elicitation: Implications for Measuring Attribute Salience and Memory Structure," in <u>Advances in Consumer Research</u>, Vol. 6, W. L. Wilkie, ed., Ann Arbor, MI: Association for Consumer Research, 269-275.

Ostrom, Thomas (1969), "The Relationship Between the Affective, Behavioral, and Cognitive Components of Attitude," <u>Journal of Experimental Social Psychology</u>, 5, 12-30.

Quillian, M. R. (1967), "Word Concepts: A Theory and Simulation of Some Basic Semantic Capabilities," <u>Behavioral Science</u>, 12, 410-430.

Thurstone, L. L. (1931), "The Measurement of Social Attitudes," <u>Journal of Abnormal and Social Psychology</u>, 26, 249-269.

Wilkie, William L. and Edgar A. Pessemier (1973), "Issues in Marketing's Use of Multi-Attribute Attitude Models," <u>Journal of Marketing Research</u>, 10, 428-441.

Zajonc, Robert B. (1980), "Feeling and Thinking: Preferences Need No Inferences," <u>American Psychologist</u>, 35, 151-175.

ATTITUDE, MOTIVATION, AND MARKETING OR
WHERE DO THE ATTRIBUTES COME FROM?

Geraldine Fennell, Fordham University, Lincoln Center, New York

ABSTRACT

Attitude researchers tend to restrict their responsibility
to studying respondents' reactions to a set of attributes, and
the relationship between attitude and behavior.   Both are
important issues.   But equally important and hitherto ignored
by attitude researchers is the question: Where do the attributes
come from?   A model of the consumer decision process is presented which contains the key elements usually studied in attitude
research namely, feelings, beliefs, and attitude as well as
attributes and their source in the person and environment
elements that motivate the brand choice decision.   It is contrasted with the Fishbein approach to studying attitude.   Implications for achieving a closer match between the marketer's
tasks and behavioral science theory and research are stated.

SOCIAL PSYCHOLOGY, CONSUMER PSYCHOLOGY, AND MARKETING RESEARCH

There are at least three interested parties for the question:
Where do the attributes come from? Social psychology, consumer
psychology, and marketing research have something to say on the
subject.   None of the three has offered what I consider to be a
complete answer by which I mean, here, an answer at the conceptual and empirical levels.   Furthermore, the answers offered by
social psychology and by marketing research are very different:
in some sense, they are mirror images of each other.

Fishbein, who represents social psychology for present purposes, tells us how to obtain a set of attributes empirically.
He states that attributes are generated by asking subjects to
list, in a free-response format, "the characteristics, qualities,
and attributes of the object, or the consequences of performing
the behavior" (Fishbein & Ajzen 1975, p. 218).

Consumer psychologists have pointed out that the question of
the theoretical source of attributes is a topic in need of attention (e.g., Cohen 1977; Pessemier & Wilkie 1972).   Cohen, for example, notes that the intellectual ancestry of the expectancy
value approach to attitude points to motivation as the source of
the attributes.   At the same time, he also notes that it is the
common practice of workers in the attitude area to "shift focus
to the object of the attitude and work back to the individual,
some as far as needs and motives (e.g., Katz 1960; Rosenberg 1956),
others (e.g., Fishbein 1965) only as far as evaluative responses

14

associated with the object through prior learning" (1977 p.2).
In their research, consumer psychologists obtain their attribute
sets in a variety of ways.   Often it is not entirely clear how
the attributes were obtained.   Authors may tell us that an
existing attribute set was used, perhaps one taken from an earlier study, or one developed by marketing research.   If Fishbein's procedure is followed, subjects are asked to state characteristics of brands, or outcomes of using a product or brand
(e.g., Ryan & Bonfield 1975, p. 122).

In marketing research once again we find an empirical procedure as we did in social psychology, but one that differs in
substantive ways from that described by Fishbein.   Qualitative
research, in particular the focus group interview, is the well-
trodden ground by which marketing research generates its attribute set, in conjunction with suggestions from the marketing
team.   Although a fair amount has been written on focus group
research, very little has been said about the model of behavior
that may direct the writing of the focus group interview guide.
By and large, marketing research texts are silent on the subject
of generating product attributes, surprisingly so in view of the
pivotal role of product attributes as the embodiment of the marketer's response to consumer wants.   The practical, if brief,
comment in Boyd, Westfall, & Stasch (1977, pp. 582-4) is a
notable exception.   How marketing research goes about generating
the attribute set has not been documented to any extent and,
perhaps for this reason, its theoretical significance has gone
unnoted.   Wilkie & Pessemier state: "Methods for attribute
generation include expert judgment and unstructered group or
depth interview" (1973, p. 428).   Note, however, that the topic
assigned to the expert judges and addressed through the unstruc-
tured interviews is different from Fishbein's direction to list
the characteristics of the attitude object.   It is to develop a
list of product attributes and benefits which consumers want in
the situation in which the attitude object (e.g., a brand) is
used.   Qualitative research starts, typically, by asking respondents to talk about the consumer activity or condition, broadly
defined, for which the brand of interest is to be used e.g., "Our
topic today is meal preparation" (cf., Wells 1974, p. 213-9).   This
is a very different procedure, empirically and conceptually, from
asking subjects to list the qualities or characteristics of brands.

In sum, social psychology and marketing research give us
different procedures for generating an attribute set and neither
appears to have considered the conceptual framework.   From consumer psychology we have some concern about conceptual under-
pinnings along with empirical procedures which reflect consumer
psychology's dual allegiance to basic psychology and to
marketing research.

Part of what I plan to do in this presentation is to des-

cribe a consumer decision model which includes the main elements
we associate with attitude models of the expectancy value variety
namely, affect, cognition, and attitude, and which also incorporates attributes and their origin in the person and environment elements that motivate the brand choice decision. Along the
way, I shall present side-by-side the approaches to attitude of
social psychology and marketing research and shall point to
substantive differences between them.

FIGURE 1: IS ATTITUDE PART OF A LARGER BEHAVIORAL MODEL?

WHERE DO THE ATTRIBUTES COME FROM?

To address the question: Where do the attributes come from?
I am going to start by asking another question: Is there a larger behavioral model in which attitude is embedded?   What are
the other concepts that come before and after attitude in a model
of behavior (Figure 1)?   One thing that may follow attitude is
behavior. The attitude-behavior relationship is tomorrow's topic
so I shall not talk in any detail about what follows attitude,
what comes to the right of Attitude in the figure, except to
remind you, in passing, of the general outlines of what is often
called the Extended Fishbein Model (Fishbein & Ajzen 1975).

FIGURE 2: A REPRESENTATION OF THE EXTENDED FISHBEIN MODEL

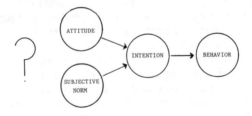

In Figure 2, Attitude and Subjective Norms combine to affect
Intention and Behavior.   At the very end of my talk I shall mention Behavior again, but until that point, the rest of what I
have to say relates to what may precede Attitude, i.e., what is
in the blank space to the left of Attitude.

The term "attitude" embodies the notion of attitude toward
something, x, the attitude object.   The attitude object, x, may
be a physical object, a concept, a behavior.   In marketing research we usually talk as though x were a brand, i.e., an <u>object</u>,
but I think it is true to say that the wording of the questions
put to survey respondents makes it clear to them that the con-

text is purchase <u>behavior</u> in a specific product category. The
attitude object, x, is represented in Figure 3, and I am asking:
How are we to conceptualize what is in the space to the left?

FIGURE 3:   RESEARCH OPERATIONS IN MARKETING RESEARCH AND
SOCIAL PSYCHOLOGY

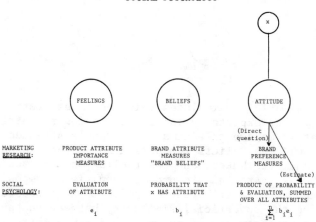

It is widely held that beliefs and feelings combine in some
way to produce attitude, so we can begin to fill the space with
the two attitude components: Beliefs and Feelings. Let's look
at the points of contact between social psychology and marketing
research practice in regard to these attitude components.

In marketing research practice probably the most frequently
asked survey questions relate to the components of attitude. Respondents are asked to rate a set of attributes for importance
when choosing a brand in the product category under study; they
are also asked to rate major brands on the same set of attributes. A direct questioning approach is usually used to obtain
overall attitude toward buying a brand, and there are many
different specific questions which are used for this purpose. In
social psychology, there are a number of versions of what is re-
ferred to in general terms as the expectancy value approach. Probably more than any other, Fishbein's has been used in consumer
psychology, and I am following Fishbein here.   Beliefs are obtained by having subjects indicate the likelihood that x, the
attitude object, has each of a number of attributes; feelings
are obtained by asking subjects to indicate the extent to which
each attribute is good or bad. The person's attitude toward the
attitude object, x, is then estimated by multiplying probability
and evaluation for each attribute and summing over the set of
attributes (Fishbein & Ajzen 1975, p. 223). Note that both in
marketing research and social psychology we cannot talk about
researching Feelings and Beliefs without using one additional
term: Attributes.

17

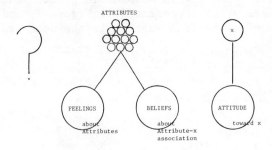

FIGURE 4: ATTRIBUTES AND ATTITUDE COMPONENTS

Our schematic now includes this additional term: Attributes
(Figure 4). The expectancy value formulation for attitude is
saying that if we are to estimate a person's Attitude toward x,
we must know: The Beliefs the person holds about associations
between x and Attributes, and the Feelings the person has about
the Attributes. Attitude toward x, then, is a composite of one's
feelings about the attributes one believes x to possess. Not-
withstanding the superficial similarity between the approaches
of social psychology and of marketing research there are crucial
differences between them. Social psychology and marketing research differ in the manner in which the attribute set is generated, in regard to the status of the attitude object, and in
their respective treatments of motivation (Figure 5).

FIGURE 5: SOME DIFFERENCES IN APPROACHES OF SOCIAL
PSYCHOLOGY AND MARKETING RESEARCH

	SOCIAL PSYCHOLOGY	MARKETING RESEARCH
ATTRIBUTE SET:	Direct request to list qualities/ characteristics of x.	Indirect approach. Built up from analysis of exploratory interviews.
ATTITUDE OBJECT(x):	Often appears as a given (e.g., The Republican Party, ERA, Going to Church).	May be created from scratch or, if it already exists, may be changed (e.g., new product, new brand, new positioning).
MOTIVATION:	Reason or context for considering x is often left ambiguous i.e., for subjects to supply their own context.	Understanding motivating influences i.e., the consumer's use-context, is of prime importance so that x may be tailored accordingly.

Specifically, with regard to the question: Where do the
attributes come from? Social psychology asks concerning the attributes which subjects believe x, the attitude object, to possess.
Marketing research uses an indirect questioning approach to identify the attributes which respondents want in the product-use
situation under study. In marketing research, then, attributes
represent consumer wants. We know that the space to the left,
in Figure 4, must contain a conceptualization of the source of
consumer wants. It must contain some representation of the
motivating influences on consumers.

One of the difficulties psychologists and others have had
with conceptualizing motivation comes, I believe, from thinking
of motivation as something that resides within the person. If

we probe deeply enough, perhaps in the deep recesses of personality, we shall find the answer to what motivates the person. As
I think marketing researchers have learned from much research on
consumer wants, elements in the person's environment as well as
elements within the person may motivate behavior, i.e., may activate behavior in a particular direction (Fennell 1975).   Accordingly, to represent motivation I shall talk about Activating
Conditions and Desired States (Figure 6).

FIGURE 6:   MOTIVATIONAL ANTECEDANTS OF ATTITUDE

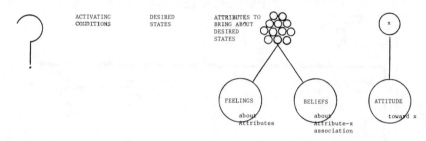

Consumers experience discomfort (Activating Condition) and
they sense a disparity between the way things are and the way
they could be (Desired State), and they may engage in behavior to
bring about the desired state (Fennell 1979a; cf., Peak 1955).
As marketers, we are interested in making available goods and
services possessing those attributes which will help consumers to
bring about their desired states.   Elsewhere (Fennell 1978), I
have described seven different kinds of activating conditions
and the direction for behavior associated with each.   Note that
the term "activating condition" allows for influences on behavior
whether from the person or the environment, and it refers to
those influences that are operating in the situation under study.

As promised, I have been working backwards from Attitude,
filling in the space to the left in the figure.   I have arrived
at the end of this enterprise, so far as our current purpose is
concerned, and what we find at the end, i.e., beyond the Activating Conditions in Figure 6, is a Person and an Environment.Where
do the attributes come from? They are the marketer's answer to
the desires of consumers which, in turn, arise from influences
coming from within the person and from the person's environment.

What we call "the environment" as though it were a unitary
entity, in fact comprises numerous systems, each one of which is
a large subject in itself.   Likewise, "the person" is composed
of many different systems, physiological and psychological, which
exist side-by-side, sometimes intersecting each other and the
environmental systems.   As marketers, we are not interested in
describing the environment _per se_, or the person _per se_, even
if it were possible to do so adequately.   What we do want to

know is how all of this enormous complexity comes together to
influence the consumer's perception of meal preparation, or household cleaning, or private transportation, or personal hygiene,
or food storage, etc.

When person systems and environment systems intersect, or
come together, as they do in different ways many times a day,
they form a Situation (Figure 7). Among the many situations

FIGURE 7: SOURCE OF ACTIVATING CONDITIONS IN PERSON AND
ENVIRONMENT ELEMENTS

ENVIRONMENT	PERSON
Physical –Natural –Built	Cognitive Units and Processes
Political	Traits

SITUATION AS PERCEIVED

Activating Conditions 1 2 3 4 5 6 7	Desired States	Desired Attributes

Economic	Values
Cultural	Self-Concept
	Skills
Societal	Interests
Family	Roles
Task	Physiology
etc.	etc.

that arise for the person in this way every day, marketers want
to understand those that involve or that may involve the use of
goods and services. I shall return shortly to fill in the rest
of this figure. First I want to examine in greater detail the
motivational and attitudinal aspects of the consumer's decision
process which are shown across the top of Figure 8: The
Activating Conditions -- "the way it is that I don't like,"
followed by Desired States -- "the way I want it to be," and
next, Desired Product Attributes -- "the attributes likely to
secure my Desired States." With regard to Brand-Attribute
Association, the consumer wants to know which brands offer and
deliver desired attributes; and finally, Overall Brand Attitude
is intended to represent the consumer's overall judgment about a
brand, taking pros and cons into account. Note that the marketplace translation of consumer wants begins with "Attributes."

Where do the attributes come from? The meeting of consumer
and producer which occurs in the translation of consumer wants
into product attributes is achieved largely through the interface
of qualitative consumer research and the technological knowledge
of the R&D department. What is going on in those countless focus
group interviews which marketing research uses to help develop

20

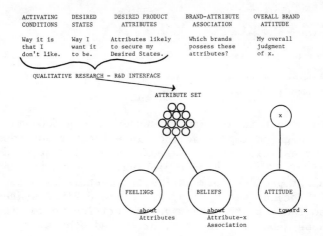

an attribute set is an attempt to get respondents to describe the elements in their own personalities and environments that provide clues to what they want in the situation under study. Note that there are two conceptually distinct phases to building the attribute set. The first has to do with understanding the consumer's perspective, i.e., activating conditions and desired states. The second has to do with translating the consumer's perspective into the physical and psychological properties of goods and services. Each phase has its own difficulties.

Understanding the Consumer's Perspective. I shall briefly mention two difficulties. First, it is a curious feature of human motivation that we seem to be able to articulate our goals more readily than our reasons for having those particular goals, or the conditions that influenced us toward the goals. In the normal course of events, this may not be any great harm although it may have something to do with the fact that often when we have achieved a long-sought goal our experience of the achievement is different from what we expected it would be. (Possibly, in set-ting our sights on that particular goal we did not choose appropriately in the light of the particular activating condi-tions which were operative.) To someone like the marketer, who is in the business of helping us to achieve our goals, our difficulty in articulating the conditions that influence us to-ward a particular goal presents a serious drawback. The problem arises because what passes as a statement of goal in everyday discourse may give little clue to the nature of its activating condition. Let's look at one example in a marketing context of the motivational ambiguity of product attributes (Fennell 1978). When people tell us for what they are striving, or what they want, they have given us minimal information about their motivation.

21

FIGURE 9:   ATTRIBUTES MAY BE MOTIVATIONALLY AMBIGUOUS

BELIEFS RELATIVE TO ACTIVATING CONDITIONS		DESIRED STATES	DESIRED ATTRIBUTES
PROBLEM SOLUTION	My dog's poor coat may be due to bad diet.	Dog's coat in good condition.	
PROBLEM PREVENTION	Dog lovers care about their pets' diet.	Evidence of my self-concept as dog lover.	Hi "importance rating" for: GOOD NUTRITION.
STABLE STATE MAINTENANCE	Basic nutrition is a routine matter.	Supplies of acceptable dog food on hand.	
EXPLORATORY INTEREST	Animal nutrition is my hobby.	News & information about nutrition.	

A respondent in a consumer survey on dog food may rate "good nutrition" high on importance, or in a focus group session on consumer orientation to pet care may say: I want good nutrition for my dog.   Without further probing, the marketer has little direction for product formulation or advertising attentional strategy. The activating conditions and desired states of consumers who indicate they want good nutrition in dog food may be any of those shown in Figure 9, or indeed others.

A second difficulty in understanding the consumer's activating conditions and desired states resides in the likelihood that in order to function in their daily lives consumers may have developed various coping strategies and defense mechanisms which serve to block from their awareness many of the larger and smaller irritations of everyday living.   Identifying these annoyances and devising ways to deal with them is one path to the promising new product idea. But how exactly is marketing to do this if the consumers to which it turns for guidance have blocked awareness of discomforts? Some twenty years ago the marketing world became disenchanted with the excesses of Freudian analysis applied to everyday products.   The possibility of subjectivity on the part of the researcher was unsettling, to say the least, when it became evident in the differing recommendations of independent researchers studying the same topic (see, for example, Ramond 1974, p. 89). Marketing moved on to other approaches to uncovering consumer wants, first to reliance on large numbers -- of respondents and data points -- made possible by computer capacity, and more recently to ever more sophisticated statistical analyses. The basic problem posed by the notion of unconscious motivation remains unresolved, and it may arise right at the time focus group respondents are supposedly sharing with us the consumer's perspective.   Dr. Nadien takes a closer look at this problem which is still very much at the frontier of known territory (Nadien 1980). At the same time, marketing has taken on the task of satisfying consumers' wants, and the possibility that people are not always able to articulate what they want comes with the territory. Marketing's practice of multi-phase interaction between consumer and producer (through the various forms of product development research) uses a fair degree of trial and error, and seems appropriate at the present stage of development in the behavioral sciences.

Translating Consumer Wants into Product Attributes. Understanding the consumer's perspective is only one of the two key
facets of building the attribute set. The other is the translation of consumer wants into product attributes. I believe most
marketing researchers would agree that it is not the respondent's
role, in qualitative research, to state the exact product features or attributes that are desired. Indeed, one of the more
common reasons why a researcher may feel dissatisfied with an
exploratory interview is that it had been hard to get the respondents to do more than playback the product attribute language
which is often used in advertising. The producer rather than
the consumer is familiar with the technology of production, and
understands what properties may and may not be built into a brand,
and how. When consumers talk in product attribute language they
are in the producer's area of expert knowledge. Consumers can
and do express reactions to product attributes, but instead of
relying on consumers to generate desired product attributes it
is preferable to have them talk about what they, and not the
producer, know at first hand namely, the conditions that give
rise to their purchase and use of products. The researcher can
facilitate translation of the consumer's perception of the product-use situation into product attributes by securing a briefing
from R&D personnel in advance of conducting exploratory interviews.
R&D people often have a wealth of information on human physiology
as well as product formulation possibilities which focus group
moderators should be acquainted with as they prepare the interview guide and moderate the discussion. With systematic preparation for the exploratory interview, the researcher is better
situated than otherwise to extract the maximum amount of useful
information. It is essential that this information be then
shared with R&D to complete the consumer-producer interface.

FIGURE 10: CONSUMERS MAY BE UNABLE TO ARTICULATE THEIR WANTS

ACTIVATING CONDITIONS	DESIRED STATES	DESIRED PRODUCT ATTRIBUTES	BRAND-ATTRIBUTE ASSOCIATION	OVERALL BRAND ATTITUDE
Way it is that I don't like.	Way I want it to be.	Attributes likely to secure my Desired States.		
(even though I may have repressed the fact I don't like it, and may not even dream that things could be otherwise).	(or would want it to be if I thought about it, or knew that I could change things).	(but don't ask me to speak product attribute language. If you do I'll playback what the advertising says. You must understand where I'm coming from and going to and what's possible technologically, and then create the attributes I want).		

For reasons such as these it is not expected that respondents in exploratory research will be in a position to give the
information marketers need in response to direct questions regarding their activating conditions, desired states or desired

product attributes. A more realistic description of the actual state of affairs is shown in Figure 10.

SITUATIONAL MODEL OF BRAND CHOICE

I turn, now, to completing my conception of the brand choice situation as perceived by the consumer, that is, standing in the consumer's shoes (Figure 11).

FIGURE 11: THE BRAND CHOICE DECISION

ENVIRONMENT	PERSON	ENVIRONMENT	PERSON

SITUATIONAL MODEL OF BRAND CHOICE BEHAVIOR

Activating
Conditions   Desired
1   State.   Desired
2   Attributes
3   Beliefs re: Brands   Buying   Brand Use   Beliefs re:
4   Attribute-   Considered   Preference   Outcome   Attribute-
5   Brand   Order for   Brand
                                       Association   Brands   Satisfactory   Association
6   Considered   Not Satisfactory
7

BEHAVIOR   CONFIRMED or REVISED
(i.e., Brand   BELIEFS (i.e.,
Purchase and Use)   Learning)

Elements in the person and in the environment combine to create an unpleasant state of affairs (Activating Condition). Unless the person uses some form of cognitive activity to neutralize the activating condition, the alternative is to engage in overt behavior. The activating condition determines the particular kinds of outcome (Desired State) and attributes (Desired Attributes) that will be positively valued by a consumer in the product-use situation under study. Drawing on what they know about the benefits and attributes that brands offer and deliver, including the minimum information that the brand is a product category member (Beliefs), consumers select for consideration those brands that seem likely to help bring about their desired states (Brands Considered). They may need some mechanism for combining their favorable and unfavorable beliefs about each brand into a single value (cf., attitude) which can then be used to rank the brands considered in terms of buying preference (Preference Ordering). Following use of the purchased brand (Brand Use Outcome), consumers judge the extent to which the brand helped to achieve their desired states and to neutralize their activating conditions. As a result of this experience, consumers' previous beliefs about the brand may have been confirmed or may need to be revised (Learning).

For example, parents see their teenage children rushing off in the morning without breakfast, and they are troubled because of their belief that good health requires starting the day with

24

a substantial meal. They may, of course, dispel their uneasiness
by questioning the soundness of the solid breakfast rule, remark-
ing perhaps to themselves that medical science, no less than other
disciplines, has its fads and that the latest medical advice may
be extolling the benefits of fasting till noon.   If cognitive
activity of this sort fails to lay their concern to rest, the
activating condition remains and it specifies the desired state
of getting some form of nutrition into their teenagers early in
the day.   How exactly this is to be done may be devised by
ingenious, caring, and diplomatic parents, but there is here an
opportunity for marketers to identify the parents' predicament
and create appropriate product forms, i.e., to translate the
essential activating elements into properties of goods and services that are responsive to the consumer's condition.

Comparison with Social Psychology's Attitude Model

Although my brand choice model contains elements that are
familiar to us from attitude research, specifically Feelings
and Beliefs, as well as Attitude itself in the sense of a summary or overall reaction to the attitude object (Figure 12), the
attitude and brand choice models differ in substantive ways. The

FIGURE 12:   ATTITUDE COMPONENTS AND THE BRAND CHOICE DECISION

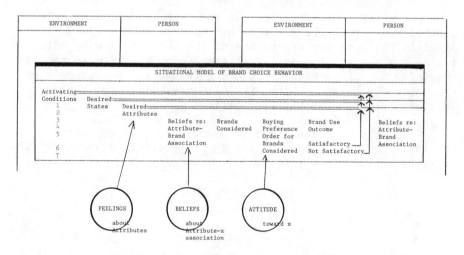

attitude model we take from social psychology starts with an
attitude object and enquires about the attributes people believe
it possesses, then enquires about people's feelings toward the
attributes.   Where do these feelings come from? What is their
source?   The answer is that we learn to have these feelings
because of other characteristics with which the attributes are
associated, which in turn are related to yet others in a chain
stretching back to early childhood:

"(attribute evaluations) are themselves a function of
beliefs linking the attribute to other characteristics and
evaluations of those characteristics. The latter evaluations are again based on beliefs and evaluations, etc. It
is possible to continue such an analysis indefinitely. Ultimately, however, one must probably fall back on hedonism,
pleasure-pain principles, or other primary motives to
account for the initial acquisition of affect. For example,
for a newborn infant ingestion of milk satisfies hunger and
may be viewed as giving pleasure or eliminating pain. Milk
thus takes on some of the pleasurable (positive) qualities
associated with hunger reduction.   In this way, a positive
attitude toward milk has been acquired.   The evaluation of
milk can now account in part for the development of
attitudes toward other objects which come to be associated
with milk (e.g., mother or breast).

        Although it is possible in principle to trace through
the development of a person's attitudes beginning with his
early childhood, it will usually be sufficient to assess
the evaluation of the attributes associated with the attitude object at a given point in time" (Fishbein & Ajzen
1975, p. 217).

For present purposes such an analysis is deficient in two
related respects.   It assumes that attributes are always evaluated in the same way regardless of the context, and by offering an explanation in historical terms only if it fails to consider
the influence of currently operating forces in the person's environment which may combine with elements within the person to
determine value in specific situations.

The attitude formulation from social psychology works
backward from an attitude object to unspecified motivations, i.e.,
activating conditions (Figure 13).   In contrast, marketing re-

FIGURE 13: ORIENTATION OF SOCIAL PSYCHOLOGY

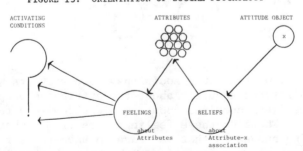

search wants to understand motivation i.e., to specify the
activating conditions, and work forward from there to an

FIGURE 14: ORIENTATION OF MARKETING RESEARCH

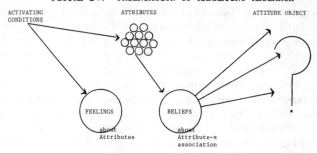

FIGURE 14: ORIENTATION OF MARKETING RESEARCH

attitude object (Figure 14). Here activating conditions endow certain attributes with value in the situations consumers find themselves in. Depending on what they know about associations between such valued attributes and ways to secure the attributes, consumers consider one or more attitude objects. Note that from the present perspective, brands, i.e., attitude objects, come up for purchase consideration if they are believed to offer desired attributes. This is in sharp contrast to the sequence of events in social psychology where the attitude object is the focus of initial attention.

In a conference sponsored by the American Marketing Association the context is clearly attitude research for marketing applications. In this spirit, then, I believe it is useful to decompose the attitude formulation and to consider the function of each of its elements in the context of a brand choice model, from the perspective of marketing, on the one hand and of psychological processes on the other (Figure 15).

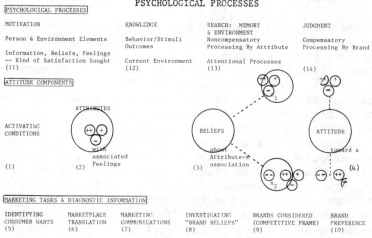

FIGURE 15: ATTITUDE COMPONENTS, MARKETING TASKS AND
PSYCHOLOGICAL PROCESSES

Elements from attitude research appear across the center of

the figure: Attributes, Feelings, Beliefs and Attitude.(1)"Activating Conditions" is added at the beginning to represent the motivating influences on consumers. (2)Rather than emphasize just Feelings, it seems more appropriate to refer to the Attributes about which consumers have Feelings. (3)"Beliefs" has a dual role: It represents consumers' information about the marketplace as well as the means by which one or more brands come up for purchase consideration. (4)Brands may not mirror consumers' desired attributes exactly, or the consumer may be choosing from two or more brands; in either case the consumer needs some means of arriving at an overall judgment that takes pros and cons into account. This may be the primary function for Attitude in the marketing application: to address the question how various pieces of information about individual options are combined to yield a value which makes it possible to order the options preferentially.

Shown across the bottom are the corresponding marketing tasks: (5)Identifying consumer wants (cf., Smith's (1956) notion of heterogeneity of demand and a market inherently segmented as regards consumer wants); (6)Translating consumer wants into the attributes of goods and services, a task that involves the collaboration of the marketing research and R&D departments; (7)Letting consumers know that a good or service is available; (8)Assessing consumers' beliefs and knowledge about brand attributes; (9)Ascertaining the particular set of brands which a consumer considers buying in order to identify the effective competitive frame for different groups of consumers (cf., buying/consideration class, Smith 1967); (10)Finally, studying consumers' buying preferences -- marketers want to know where their brand places in the buying preference ordering of the brands consumers have considered.

Shown across the top of Figure 15 are the major psychological processes which we would study in order to understand the determinants of each component of the consumer's brand choice decision. (11)Activating conditions arise from elements in the person and the person's environment. They originate from an interplay among, for example, information, beliefs, and feelings, which determines the kind of satisfaction the consumer seeks. (12)What consumers do to neutralize their activating conditions depends in part on their store of knowledge and belief about the outcomes associated with various behaviors and stimuli as well as their knowledge of the possibilities offered by the current environment. (13)In generating specific action possibilities (e.g., brands to buy) consumers presumably search their memory and the current environment, and likely use noncompensatory processing by attribute in this search stage. Consumers' scanning of the environment takes place intentionally and incidentally, possibly using a mechanism that lowers the threshold for reception of affectively relevant stimulation (cf., affective determinants of attention allocation, Fennell 1979b). Finally, in the judgment phase, the consumer may use compensatory processing by brand to convert the strengths and weaknesses of each option being considered into a single value.

IMPLICATIONS

My analysis of consumer decision processes suggests a number of conceptual distinctions and implications for attitude research which, because of space limitations, I can touch only briefly here (Figure 16).   First, there are the related issues

FIGURE 16: SUMMARY

To answer the question I began with: Where do the attributes come from?

- The variables we study in attitude research are part of a larger model of behavior.
- This larger behavioral model has motivational and information processing aspects.
- The attributes we study in marketing originate in the motivational aspects of the model. Specifically, they are the qualities of goods and services that help consumers to achieve Desired States and to neutralize Activating Conditions.

As for Attitude, Motivation, and Marketing:

- It is Motivation's job to explain the kinds of satisfaction consumers seek.
- It is Attitude's job to explain how consumers choose among options they are considering in order to realize the satisfactions they seek.
- It is Marketing's job to make options available with attributes that deliver consumer satisfaction.

Some Conceptual Distinctions:

- Motivational, Search, and Judgment aspects of the decision process.
- Judgment and Affect aspects of the attitude construct.
- Beliefs and Knowledge and the nature of accompanying Affect.

Some Implications of Marketing Research practice for Multi-Attribute Attitude Research:

Since Attributes reflect subjects' wants --

- Generate attributes from subjects' reactions to the entire product-use situation rather than to the attitude object only.
- Use subjects who engage in the relevant consumer activity in place of asking subjects to pretend they are in the market.
- Remember heterogeneity of demand and don't expect all subjects to show a common pattern of performance.
- Because attributes are motivationally ambiguous, study activating conditions as well as consumer reactions to product attributes.

of the necessity for making a distinction between belief and knowledge, and the question whether or not affect precedes behavior.   Attitude is often understood to mean a behavioral tendency to approach or withdraw from an attitude object with accompanying feelings of favorableness/unfavorableness, or liking/disliking.   Certainly, the quality of this feeling is likely to be different when the attitude object is known only by description (belief) and when it is known by experience (knowledge).   Marketing research practice acknowledges the distinction between knowledge with and without experience when "brand beliefs" data, for example, are analyzed separately for triers and nontriers.

In my brand choice model, feeling originates in the motivational processes of the consumer and directs the consumer's search for appropriate attributes.   If one brand only comes up for consideration as possessing the desired attribute, it may be bought on the basis of the consumer's belief alone.   It seems unnecessary to postulate that the consumer likes the brand in advance of trying the brand. If the brand delivers on its claim, the consumer may well like it after use. However, if we apply the Fishbein formula in the case just described, based on what the consumer believes about the brand and how the consumer evaluates what is believed, we obtain a measure of attitude, or liking for the brand, in advance of purchase. The Fishbein approach appears to force us to make an unwarranted assumption about liking (affect) in advance of experience. Even in cases where the consumer is using judgment processes, e.g., assessing pros and cons of one or more brands, it seems preferable to consider two issues separately: 1) the particular combinatorial rules and trade off systems that yield an ordering of the options which are being considered: 2) the subject of affect -- whether and where it occurs in the decision process, and its specific nature.

Whether affect occurs before or after behavior (e.g.. brand purchase) is. of course, an issue that has arisen in the discussion relative to the hierarchy of advertising effects (e.g., Ramond 1974, pp. 14-22; Ray 1973). My analysis here suggests additional questions about the way advertising works that are, perhaps, even more interesting. Does advertising merely supply information (e.g., about brand-attribute associations) and rely on existing consumer affect to power the purchase decision, so to speak, or are there circumstances in which it supplies both information and motive power for the purchase decision? Advertising, for example, could create liking for an item in advance of purchase so that the nonpossession of the item becomes an activating condition for the consumer. Also, it could inculcate a belief which combines with existing person and environment elements to create an activating condition, at the same time creating an appropriate brand-attribute association so that the consumer selects the advertised brand as the means of neutralizing the activating condition.

Underlying what has been suggested so far is the further implication that the consumer's degree of familiarity with a particular motivating situation is an important variable with theoretical ramifications that go beyond those so far articulated in discussions of Howard's (e.g.. 1977) or Robinson, Faris, & Wind's (1968) threefold classification of buying situations. The dimensions that define familiarity may vary depending on the marketing task being studied. My analysis of consumer decision processes, for example, suggests the importance of distinguishing between instances in which the consumer's information about the marketplace is based on experience and those in which it is not, a qualitative distinction with theoretical implications that are not apparent when amount rather than kind of information is stressed.

With regard to the implications for attitude research which is conducted in the consumer psychology laboratory with an eye to marketing applications, a "strong" interpretation of what I have been saying is that the kinds of questions typically addressed in multi-attribute, multi-brand research are meaningful only in the context of a decision process originating in consumer wants. Marketing researchers recognise the motivational context by means of a number of procedures which often are absent in laboratory research. First, some consumer psychologists have noted subjects' difficulty in articulating desired attributes (e.g., Mazis, Ahtola, & Klippel 1975, pp. 46-7). Generating the attribute set in a manner similar to that used in marketing research may be helpful (i.e., from a discussion in which subjects' reaction to the entire product-use situation is obtained rather than only to the attitude object or the behavioral outcomes). Second, marketing researchers screen respondents to obtain those currently engaging in the consumer activity of interest. In the absence of evidence that subjects who are asked to pretend they are in the market for a particular product behave in a manner substantially similar to subjects who truly have relevant wants, the marketing research screening practice appears preferable for use in the laboratory as well. Third, because of the origin of attributes in consumer wants, attitude researchers may consider the implications of heterogeneity in demand for their research. Fourth, because product attributes are motivationally ambiguous (i.e., the "same" product attribute may be desired by consumers with differing activating conditions), consumer psychologists may expect to reach a better understanding of consumer behavior when their analysis is differentiated at the level of activating conditions rather than at the level of product attributes only in the manner of multi-attribute, multi-brand research. The last two points suggest an initial clustering of subjects in the manner of segmentation research.

Finally, systematically relevant information is lost when, instead of ascertaining the brands they consider buying, subjects are required to react to a predetermined set of brands. The information lost is of great significance in a marketing context and, more basically, an important aspect of the decision process is removed from investigation namely, the emergence of candidate behaviors and stimuli for consideration in specific situations.

In a context where the motivational, search, and judgment aspects of the decision process are distinguished, the attitude research tradition may contribute primarily to elucidating the judgment aspect, i.e., the processes by which consumers reconcile what they want and what they know in choosing among the options they are considering. Progress to this end will be facilitated by research which is integrated within the framework of the entire decision process.

REFERENCES

Boyd, Harper W., Ralph Westfall, and Stanley Stasch (1977), Marketing Research: Text and Cases. 4th edition. Homewood. IL: Irwin.

Cohen, Joel B. (1977), "The Structure of Product Attributes: Defining Attribute Dimensions for Planning and Evaluation," paper presented at an American Marketing Association/Marketing Science Institute Workshop on Analytic Approaches to Product and Marketing Planning, University of Pittsburg, November 18.

Fennell, Geraldine (1975) "Motivation Research Revisited," Journal of Advertising Research, 15 (June), 23-28.

_____ (1978), "Consumers' Perception of the Product-Use Situation," Journal of Marketing, 42 (April), 38-47.

_____ (1979a), "The Situation," working paper #114, Department of Social Sciences, Fordham Univeristy, Lincoln Center.

_____ (1979b), "Attention Engagement," in Current Issues and Research in advertising, James L. Leigh and Claud R. Martin, eds., Ann Arbor: University of Michigan, Graduate School of Business Admininstration.

Fishbein, Martin (1965), "A Consideration of Beliefs, Attitudes, and Their Relationship," in Current Studies in Social Psychology, Ivan D. Steiner and Martin Fishbein, eds., New York: Holt, Rinehart & Winston.

_____, and I. Ajzen (1975), Belief, Attitude, Intention, and Behavior: An Introduction to Theory and Research, Reading, MA: Addison-Wesley.

Howard, John A. (1977), Consumer Behavior: Application of Theory, New York: McGraw-Hill.

Katz, Daniel (1960), "The Functional Approach to the Study of Attitudes," Public Opinion Quarterly, 24 (Summer), 163-204.

Mazis, M. B., O. T. Ahtola, and R. E. Klippel (1975), "A Comparison of Four Multi-Attribute Models in the Prediction of Consumer Attitudes," Journal of Consumer Research, 2 (June), 38-52.

Nadien, Margot (1980), "Coping and Defending: Guidelines for Research with Psychologically Naive Respondents," in Proceedings of 11th Annual Attitude Conference, Richard W. Olshavsky,

32

ed., Chicago: American Marketing Association.

Peak, Helen (1955), "Attitude and Motivation," in Nebraska Sym-
posium on Motivation, M. R. Jones, ed., Lincoln: University
of Nebraska Press.

Pessemier, Edgar A. and William Wilkie (1972), "Multi-Attribute
Choice Theory -- A Review and Analysis," working paper #372,
Institute for Research in the Behavioral, Economic and Manage-
ment Sciences, Lafayette, Indiana: Purdue University.

Ramond, Charles (1974), The Art of Using Science in Marketing,
New York: Harper & Row.

_____ (1976), Advertising Research: The State of the
Art, New York: Association of National Advertisers.

Ray, Michael (1973), "Marketing Communication and the Hierarchy
of Effects," in New Models for Communication Research, Peter
Clarke, ed., Beverly Hills: Sage.

Rosenberg, Milton (1956), "Cognitive Structure and Attitudinal
Affect," Journal of Abnormal and Social Psychology, 53
(November), 367-72.

Ryan, Michael J. and E. H. Bonfield (1975), "The Fishbein
Extended Model and Consumer Behavior," Journal of Consumer
Research, 2 (September), 118-35.

Smith, Gail (1967), "How GM Measures Ad Effectiveness," in
Readings in Market Research, Keith K. Cox, ed., New York:
Appleton-Century-Crofts.

Smith, Wendell (1956), "Product Differentiation and Market Segmentation as Alternative Marketing Strategies," Journal of
Marketing, 20 (July), 3-8.

Wells, William D. (1974), "Group Interviewing," in Handbook of
Marketing Research, Robert Ferber, ed., New York: McGraw-Hill.

Wilkie, William L. and Edgar A. Pessemier (1973), "Issues in
Marketing's Use of Multi-Attribute Attitude Models," Journal
of Marketing Research, 10 (November), 428-41.

COPING AND DEFENDING: GUIDELINES FOR EXPLORATORY RESEARCH WITH PSYCHOLOGICALLY NAIVE RESPONDENTS

Margot B. Nadien, Fordham University, New York

ABSTRACT

Marketers' efforts to identify consumer wants may be imped-
ed by the presence in qualitative research of defenders, that
is, of respondents who cannot consciously recognize or communicate their true desires because they have forced their desires
into unconsciousness. Methods are suggested for detecting and
counteracting the misleading effects of certain defenses.

INTRODUCTION

In seeking to identify and satisfy human wants, marketers
rely in part upon the consciously expressed desires of respondents during exploratory or "qualitative" research, with such information serving as one basis for generating ideas for new
products. At the same time, psychology places before us the notion of unconscious motivation, thereby suggesting that information yielded by qualitative research may be flawed because, a-
mong other reasons, some consumers may be unable to articulate
their true wants (Fennell 1980).

Consider the following state of affairs. Before marketing
creates remedies, many people uncomplainingly tolerate a host of
minor irritations and discomforts, often viewing them as an in-
evitable part of the human condition. They stoically endure
such discomforts as the pain of adhesive tapes being ripped from
their skin; the sting of alcohol or iodine being applied to
wounds; the bitter chalky taste of antacids; the itching from
dandruff and athlete's foot; the anxiety caused when having to
swallow oversized pills; and the distastefulness of gritty,
pasty-textured dentifrice. People deal with these and similar
discomforts in one of two ways. Those who are "copers" retain
conscious awareness of their discomforts but do not voice them,
continuing to tolerate them until alerted to the existence of
such remedies as "the ouchless band-aid," liquid medications in
place of pills, anodynes for itchy scalps and feet, and the sensory pleasure of gel dentifrice or pleasantly flavored antacids.
Those who are "defenders," however, use a different strategy.
Instead of silently but consciously enduring minor discomforts,
they immediately blot them out of consciousness. This second
type of response frequently traces to an ingrained childhood
habit of defending against pain by banishing it out of conscious-

34

ness (Wells and Beard 1973). Once established, this defensive method tends to generalize to a wide range of situations, even to ones involving the minor pains of everyday life. Thus, when remedies for daily discomforts are created, defenders may ignore them because they have dismissed from consciousness all awareness of the conditions for which such remedies were devised.

Let us return now to the issue of developing information about consumer wants during qualitative research. If both types of individuals, copers and defenders, are part of a focus group study, only the copers can be relied on to voice their true wants. The defenders, by virtue of habitually forcing their unpleasant feelings and desires into unconsciousness, probably do not recognize their true motives and, hence, may fail to communicate them. The presence of defenders may thus subvert the marketer's goal of identifying consumer wants.

Can anything be done to help researchers deal with the possible presence of defenders in qualitative research? Moderators may perhaps find it helpful if they had guidelines for identifying defenders and, possibly, for even discovering their unconscious wants.

This paper, then, has a twofold purpose. One is to note ways in which moderators may recognize defenders. The second is to suggest a possible method whereby moderators may penetrate beneath some defenses so as to uncover a defender's true but unconscious desires.

EGO DEFENSE MECHANISMS

Before noting how moderators may identify and deal with respondents who cannot recognize and articulate their true consumer desires, let us briefly review some reasons why consumer wishes may operate unconsciously rather than consciously.

When conceptualized in Freudian terms, all desires, including consumer wants, could be said to represent direct or indirect expressions of initially unconscious wishes for biological need satisfaction. These wishes arise out of our id, that aspect of our personality which is innate and which operates throughout life in an unchanging and unconscious manner. The conscious recognition of our desires, and the ability to discover realistic and nondestructive ways of satisfying those desires, comes about only by means of the development of our ego, the rational and adaptive facet of our personality. However, during childhood, several obstacles may inhibit our ego's aim of satisfying our consumer and other wishes. One obstacle could be the overdevelopment of a third part of our personality, our superego, whose

acquired ideals and lofty moral aims may oppose the realization
of fundamental id desires. Conscious wishes may also be thwart-
ed if they are opposed and censured by significant authorities
(parents) and peers, and sometimes, too, if there are no realistic opportunities for their satisfaction.

When conflicts arise between innate id desires, on the one
hand, and on the other, opposition by our superego, by realistic obstacles or by disapproving social figures, we experience
frustration; and if that frustration is intolerable, our ego
steps in and protects us from consciously experiencing the frustration. This is achieved through our defense mechanisms--i.e.,
differing strategies our ego uses to force out of consciousness
and into unconsciousness painful psychological states.

The outcome of using defense mechanisms may initially be a-
daptive. Defense mechanisms may prevent our experiencing severe
or prolonged pain, which can be psychologically harmful. If
perpetuated into adulthood, however, ego defenses may prove inappropriate and maladaptive by virtue of becoming habitual and
of generalizing to any situation involving the mere expectation
of unpleasant conscious states, even ones entailing only minor
discomforts. Certainly, in terms of qualitative research, habitual and inappropriate defenders may impede the moderator's
attempt to uncover consumer desires, particularly ones related
to eliminating sources of discomfort. The opportunity to develop remedies for discomforts arises only if the discomforts themselves are first identified.

The Use of Defense Mechanisms in Focus Group Research

There are a host of defense mechanisms people may develop
in order to avoid conscious awareness of uncomfortable or painful states. Some of the most frequently used ones are repression, denial, reaction formation, projection, sublimation, fix-
ation and regression, rationalization, intellectualization, as-
ceticism, and uniformism. I shall deal only with repression,
denial, reaction formation and projection; for these are the ego
defenses which are more likely to disguise or distort the unconscious consumer wants of some respondents during qualitative research. Each of these defenses will be considered in terms of
the reason for its development, its operation, and its possible
manifestations in qualitative research--in this case, focus
group discussions of floor cleaning and waxing.

Repression. Because it functions not only as a separate defense but also as an aspect of all other defenses, repression is
the chief defense mechanism. It consists in the forcing out of
consciousness and into unconsciousness those wishes, feelings,
thoughts, or memories that are too painful to be endured at a
conscious level. In terms of a focus group discussion of effort-

less alternatives to floor waxes, habitual repressors may have repressed awareness of the arduousness involved in floor waxing. Thus, when asked about easier alternatives to maintaining shiny floors, repressors may appear completely nonresponsive, manifesting their seeming indifference in terms of blank facial expressions or the shrugging of their shoulders.

Denial. Intolerable experiences of frustration or pain sometimes threaten to break through simple repression. When this is the case, a person may resort to the defense mechanism of denial by first repressing the unpleasant or painful conscious experiences and then by superimposing the further protection of consciously denying that which is unconsciously true. Accordingly, habitual deniers may disguise an unconscious dislike of the effort involved in floor cleaning and waxing by indignantly denying that they experience any effort whatsoever. Deniers might thus be seen to shake vigorously their heads at the suggestion of less effortful alternatives to floor waxing and might be heard to insist that "floor care is easy" or "floor waxing is a cinch...There's nothing to it."

Reaction formation. While denial and repression are strong defenses, reaction formation is an even more formidable one. It may develop if conscious states (desires, thoughts and feelings) violate cherished personal or social values and thus carry the threat of self-condemnation or condemnation by significant others. To avoid this intolerable pain, the disapproved attitudes are first repressed. Then, as an additional protection against disapproved desires seeping back into conscious thought and behavior, one consciously experiences and expresses that which accords with one's personally or socially approved values--i.e., the exact opposite of one's true and unconscious desires. Habitual users of reaction formation, particularly persons who believe one should never flinch from hard or unpleasant tasks, might insist that they simply "adore" hard work. Or, they may strongly argue that effortless alternatives would deprive them of the joy of achieving beauty in their home primarily through their own effort and hard work.

Incidentally, those using reaction formation may betray their unconscious desires or feelings in one of two ways. They may make a verbal slip, unintentionally gushing about how much they "hate" hard work when they actually intended (and thought) they had said that they "adore" it. Or they may reveal their unconscious attitudes by exaggerated and obsessive responses. In other words, reaction-formation behavior often represents a case of "the lady doth protest too much."

Projection. Like reaction formation, the defense mechanism of projection is activated by conscious wishes, feelings or

thoughts which violate one's own standards or those of significant others. However, while reaction formation is a self-puni-
tive mechanism, projection is destructive of others and is char-
acterized by a need to avoid experiencing the guilt (i.e., self-
punishment) that is aroused by wishes, feelings or thoughts
which one personally disapproved. In projection, one's own disapproved and guilty states are first repressed and then projected onto others. Thereafter, one seeks to punish these others
for the attitudes that one has attributed to them.

Habitual users of projection may strongly castigate those
who object to the effortfulness of using floor cleansing and
waxing agents. In other words, projection represents a case of
"the pot calling the kettle black" in that projectors seek to
denounce and punish others for the very attitudes of which they
themselves feel guilty and deserving of punishment.

Before discussing what marketers could do to offset the
misleading responses of defenders in focus group studies, let me
caution that behaviors described as reflective of a given defense could, in a few instances, be mirroring the true attitudes
of copers. Thus, a useful guideline for distinguishing the expression of a coper's true wants from a defender's disguised or
distorted wants is to remember that defensive behavior is often
inappropriate--i.e., reactions are unusually intense or indig-
nant or insistent or repetitive or, at the very least, are contrary to what one might normally expect.

OFFSETTING THE EFFECTS OF DEFENDERS' DEFENSES

Thus far, I have noted ways in which skillful moderators
may recognize respondents who may be using defense mechanisms in
focus group research. However, marketers would probably want to
know what practical steps they could take to offset the possibly
misleading findings of studies in which defenders represent a
sizable proportion of the respondents.

Obviously, one approach would be for moderators merely to
be cognizant of the possible presence of defenders and to make
some allowance for their responses when evaluating the findings
of the qualitative research. However, a more desirable approach
would be to find methods of penetrating beneath the defenses so
as to discover the defenders' true but unconscious wants.

Is such an approach possible? Owing to the absence of research on defenders as respondents, psychologists can merely offer some suggestions that could be explored. To begin with,
psychologists would caution that all defenses are difficult to
abolish; and this is particularly true in the case of reaction

formation and projection, mechanisms that are so deeply embedded in the personality as to be resistant to eradication except by means of some form of therapy. On the other hand, the less deeply rooted defenses of repression and denial may be discarded once one discovers through reality testing that, within specific situations, there is no longer any realistic reason for using such defensive reactions (Hall and Lindzey 1978). Thus, it may well be possible to probe beneath the defense mechanisms of repression and denial during qualitative research.

A Possible Approach to Dismantling Some Defenses

One approach to dismantling the defenses of repressors and deniers during a focus group study draws on our understanding of the origin and purpose of defenses. As noted earlier, defenses usually originate in intolerable childhood frustration occasioned by two mutually exclusive goals: the satisfaction of fundamental innate needs--ones whose gratification affords physical comfort and the avoidance of physical discomfort--and the competing and stronger goal of satisfying acquired social needs of approval by significant authorities and peers through conformity to societal standards which oppose the immediate or direct satisfaction of fundamental needs. When such a conflict results in abandonment of fundamental need gratification, sometimes one experiences a degree of tension and pain which cannot be tolerated and which is therefore forced out of consciousness.

When this has been the basis for repression and denial, one strategy for moderators would be to suggest that conformity to the standards of significant figures no longer requires sacrificing physical comfort and enduring physical discomfort.

How might such a strategy be achieved during a focus group interview? One possibility would be for moderators to suggest that persons comparable to significant childhood figures currently approve the expression of those very unconscious wishes, feelings and thoughts against which the respondents are now defending, with such approval stemming from the present view that "acknowledging and catering to minor discomforts enables the conservation of energies for more important activities than merely tolerating everyday discomforts." Statements comparable to this one might enable defenders to recognize that the original reason for their defenses no longer exists and, hence, that repression or denial of the minor discomforts of everyday life is no longer necessary.

How might such an approach be implemented? One way would be for moderators to cite significant figures that are tailor-made for the particular respondents in that group session. This could be done by administering a pre-session questionnaire in which respondents would give information about the specific fig-

ures that are currently important to them. An alternative and
clearly less troublesome approach would be to develop and have
available an all-purpose list of "significant individuals"--i.e.,
persons adjudged to be recognized authorities or prestigious
persons for people-at-large.

Methods of Counteracting Deeply Entrenched Defenses

As mentioned earlier, it seems unlikely that moderators
could successfully reach persons defending against unconscious
consumer wants through deeply ingrained protections of reaction
formation or projection. In such cases, moderators can merely
be sensitive to the possible presence of such respondents, with
a view to assessing their comments accordingly.

The fact that there is no known method of penetrating beneath such stubborn defenses as reaction formation and projection also suggests the advisability of not relying solely on
qualitative research for identifying consumer wants. Indeed, it
underscores the wisdom of marketers' current practice of studying consumer wants by utilizing the full spectrum of product-
development research methods, including not only focus groups,
but also in-home placement tests, small-scale test-marketing,
and similar methods.

REFERENCES

Fennell, Geraldine (1980), "Attitude, Motivation and Marketing
or Where do the Attributes Come From?" in Richard W. Olshavsky,
ed., Proceedings of the 11th Attitude Research, Chicago:
American Marketing Association.

Hall, Calvin and Gardner Lindzey (1978), Theories of Personality, 3rd ed., New York: John Wiley & Sons.

Wells, William and Arthur Beard (1973), "Personality and Consumer Behavior," in Scott Ward and Thomas Robertson, eds.,
Consumer Behavior, Englewood Cliffs, NJ: Prentice-Hall, Inc.

BRAIN WAVE ANALYSIS IN ATTITUDE
RESEARCH: PAST, PRESENT AND FUTURE

Sidney Weinstein
NeuroCommunication Research Laboratories, Danbury

ABSTRACT

The history of brainwave analysis in marketing, advertising, and media research began in 1969 with a study performed in collaboration with Dr. Herbert Krugman. Numerous
publications have since related brainwave analysis to psychological attributes such as: recall, recognition, interest involvement, motivation, etc. during study of radio and television
commercials and programming, newspaper and magazine advertising,
package design, etc. The decade of the '80s will show an increased use of this method.

INTRODUCTION

Because of the increasing popularity of brain wave analysis over the last decade, and the frequency of published literature on the subject, I will assume that you are familiar with
the methodology and not discuss it. This will leave us time
to discuss the potential applications to marketing and advertising research   (Krugman 1977; 1978a,b; Weinstein 1978a, b, d).

The use of brain wave analysis in marketing and advertising research has undergone a development similar to that of
most new scientific phenomena. The first stage, analogous to
Krugman's theory on first seeing a commercial, was "What is a
brain wave?" The second stage, "What about it?" comprised
research on validity, reliability, precision, etc. The stage
to which we have now progressed is concerned with the specific
of application.

Numerous studies have been performed in the past decade
dealing with many of the practical problems encountered by advertisers, advertising agencies, research organizations concerned with a specific medium, and large organizations which
produce films for entertainment. Most of these studies were
conducted under agreements which preclude divulging the results,
I am, however, permitted to mask the identities and will discuss
some results. For other studies, the sponsors have published
the data alone or in collaboration with my colleagues and me,
and I will cite these results, too. Chronologically primary

among these are the studies of Herb Krugman, Leo Bogart and Stu Tolley which were initiated in 1969.

I would like to correct an error of reporting which describes Krugman's first report on brain waves which appeared in the February, 1971 issue of the Journal of Advertising Research. The Los Angeles reporter (Siegal 1979) stated it was Krugman's secretary who was tested; in actuality, it was my secretary. This is not so trivial a point as it may appear, since questions are often raised concerning the effect of laboratory setting on the brain waves of a naive person. Since my secretary had seen the equipment being used daily for years, being tested again was not an unusual occurrence for her. Since that time, we have learned that naive subjects will show slightly different brain waves, but only for a short time until they habituate to the surroundings. Although the setting does not contribute to the production of unusual brain waves, our TV screening rooms now look like movie theaters, not laboratories.

Let me remind you briefly of some of the findings of this early paper. (1) The subject's mode of brain wave response differed more between print and TV than it did to content differences within the commercials. (2) The brain's response to print was more active than it was to TV. (3) Repeated exposure to a commercial showed either continual diminution of the Beta wave (the one concerned with activation or involvement), or a peak at the second exposure of the commercial, followed by a drop at the third, but still sustaining what Krugman called "a little life...even in what appears to be a satiated condition."

Interest in these results generated the desire to do additional studies, and Leo Bogart and Stu Tolley of the Newspaper Advertising Bureau also collaborated with us on another pilot study. Stu Tolley reported some of the results at the 1976 Convention of the American Psychological Association, in Washington, D. C. Although there were many interesting findings reported, the one that stands out deals with the emotional significance of the stimuli. Even with a sample of only three subjects, he reported a statistically significant enhancement of beta activity for "significant" in contrast to "emotionally neutral material." As Tolley put it "we seem to have documented that when someone is actively processing something emotionally significant in either [newspapers or TV], there is a rather unique EEG pattern that seems to run across subjects, regardless of individual differences. On the other hand, when a person is processing something in the media that he or she does not consider to be of any particular emotional significance, then much more of the person's time is dominated by waves in the low alpha range..." (1979).

In the decade since this early research we have learned a
great deal about how to use brain wave analysis for practical
purposes, and have been able to add generically to the field of
information in the area, as well to solve specific problems in
advertising, marketing, etc.

Permit me to cite a few results from subsequent studies.
In the ARF conference in 1978, Krugman reported several highly
interesting results derived from our brain wave analysis of a
family of "Edison" commercials. (1) Print "supers" always split
the audience. That is, each person reacts to the print with his
right hemisphere. The same commercial is seen by some, read by
others, heard as words by some, heard as auditory images by
others. (2) The use of "voice-over" in a commercial diminishes
the intensity of the brain's response. (3) Logos, and spoken
names of unknown people produce not left but right brain responses: "familiar names, with attendant associations get left
responses." (4) Ideas which create thoughts cause left brain
responses, as when the character Edison mentions "I've been deaf
since I was 12 years old." (5) Imagined scenes which are produced by spoken stories produce right brain responses--but if
they also deal in ideas, the left brain responds as well.

Krugman concluded that a "virtue of the present research
lies in the demonstrated ability to identify which media content
creates thinking and which creates imagery without thought. In
the past the latter, which is so to speak, 'silent,' has not
been available for study by the techniques of verbal questioning
or interviewing as we have known them"(1978a).

In the August issue of the Journal of Advertising Research,
we reported a study sponsored by Time, Newsweek, Readers Digest,
TV Guide, and Family Circle which analyzed the effect on brain
waves of 30 commercials (Appel, Weinstein, and Weinstein 1979).
There were 10 brands, each represented by one known high recall
and one known low recall commercial. These were all tested at
the one, two, and three exposure level for degree of beta activity. The average amount of brain activity for the high recall
commercials was significantly (25%) greater than the average
amount of brain activity for the low recall commercials. When
the average levels of brain activity are examined separately for
the three exposures of the low and high recall commercials it is
apparent that the second exposure of each type produced the
greatest amount of brain activity, and the third exposure the
least. These data confirm Krugman's conclusions that most evaluation of the message occurs on the second exposure. It also
suggests that the first two exposures may work synergistically
such that the first exposure prepares the brain for the second
one, which involves the greatest message evaluation. A potential
implication for media is that two insertions of a new commercial
in a single program may provide a rapid synergy.

A subsequent follow-up intermedia study sponsored by the same five magazines, and dealing with recall of print ads and television commercials (Weinstein, Appel, and Weinstein 1980) again confirmed the early finding of Krugman that magazine ads produce significantly higher levels of Beta activity than do TV commercials. Furthermore, a confirming, significant, positive relationship was observed between levels of unaided brand recall and total brain activity. The correlation between brain activity and brand recall levels was +.76.

We performed another intermedia study for the Radio Advertising Bureau (Weinstein 1979c) in which we studied brain waves of 100 subjects using 18 radio commercials and 2 paired TV commercials. The results for paired Radio and TV commercials showed: (1) that radio commercials produced higher indices of brain activity than the paired TV commercials, (2) TV tended to show greater activity on the right, whereas Radio tended to show greater activity on the left. (3) For TV, verbal ratings were greater than the brain wave measures, whereas for radio the opposite was the case. This indicates that the traditional verbal responses for TV may be exaggerated, whereas those for radio may be underestimated. (4) In the same study, we found that TV version often scored quite a bit higher in the brain wave measures if the subject had already heard the radio version of the same commercial. However, when TV was exposed first, brain waves for radio were only slightly enhanced in the second position. This finding suggests to me that people were imagining a visual scene to accompany the radio spot, and when the TV commercial occurred, their brains would actively compare the imagined visual and the actual TV commercial, causing increased brain activity to register during viewing of the TV spot. When TV was presented first, the subject's brain registered recognition during the radio spot, but the active comparison of imagined versus actual visuals did not take place, and the brain excitation levels were not enhanced as much. The implication of this finding is that a new TV campaign might benefit from a warmup run in radio for a month or so before the TV breaks.

These samples of early and recent results were taken from published studies. Even more numerous studies dealing with proprietary data have also yielded intriguing results. Among these were comparative studies of umbrella versus line commercials; studies designed to select a spokesperson for a large corporation; studies to select concepts to employ in commercials; casting studies designed to select the most interesting performer for a television program; studies of magazine covers, book cover designs, and print ads to select the proper positioning and design characteristics; studies of full length television programs to predict potential success; studies of the impact of musical compositions or of musical accompaniment to commercials.

Let's consider some of the results obtained for the actual
situations. A study of umbrella versus line commercials was
done in a single study in a target group of 100 whose characteristics indicated that they were potential purchasers of the
product. Although the executions were quite similar in that we
were dealing with very rough versions, the results clearly
demonstrated unanimous superiority of all the line over the
umbrella commercials. The subjects were obviously more interested in the specific product than in the company which produced
them.

A large agency was interested in selecting a spokesperson
to replace a well known one if the need should arise. Film
clips of some 25 candidates were shown to a target group of 100
potential users of the service advertised. The results provided
four distinct groups, from highly interesting to little or no
interest. Adjective check lists were applied to the top group
to determine whether their potential as interesting individuals
conformed to the characteristics the client would find desirable.

Let's consider one more of the studies; one concerned with
selecting a performer for a prime time television show. Some 20
personalities, performers, etc. were shown on video tape to a
group of 300 randomly selected subjects while brain waves were
recorded. Rankings for the performers on these brain waves were
obtained separately for the men and women. One performer ranked
first for men and third for women. An earlier study using verbal responses alone however, had ranked this performer much
lower. The decision was made by the client to ignore the con-
flicting brain wave data, to accept the verbal results, and not
hire the performer. Several months later, a rival organization
starred this performer with some success. The subsequent conclusion expressed by those who made the prior decision was that
perhaps controversial performers can more validly be assessed
by means of brain waves than by conscious, verbal methods.

We have considered the past and some of the present of brain
wave analysis. Now let us briefly consider a little of the
future that we have already embarked on. We believe that it is
important to interrelate marketing decisions, product development, and advertising effectiveness in a single program. This
program will first evaluate the appropriateness of marketing
decisions vis a vis a new product for a planned target group.
The second stage will deal with the appropriateness of the actual
product for the target group, and the third stage will deal with
the efficacy of the commercials for the product in the same group.

Let us consider how the approach may be applied to a single
product, fragrances. The first stage is to define the characteristics of various target prototypes, for example, sensual-

romantic-seductive, sophisticated-rich-chic, sporty-out-doors, and career oriented-independent. Once selected, brain wave analysis is used to match specific fragrances to these prototype women. The final stage assesses the brain waves obtained while exposing them to commercials, print ads and package designs for the specific fragrances. This plan is only one of the many potential applications of brain wave analysis that we will see in the future decade.

I believe I have demonstrated why we agree with Krugman's conclusions concerning the value of brain wave analysis. He said "Ultimately...I have to look to brain measures. It is here where the great capacities lie. It is here where the selection mechanisms operate. This is where the action is, and can be measured—during deepest sleep, during drowsy or hypnotic states all the way up to wild excitement..."(1978b).

Since it is apparent that the conclusions obtained by using this method could not have been obtained using any of the usual methods, we believe that the decade of the eighties will show an exponential increase in the application of brain wave analysis in the marketing and advertising areas.

REFERENCES

Appel, Valentine, Sidney Weinstein and Curt Weinstein (1979), "Brain Activity and Recall of TV Advertising," Journal of Advertising Research, 19 (August), 7-15.

Krugman, Herbert E. (1971), "Brain Wave Measures of Media Involvement," Journal of Advertising Research, 11 (February), 3-10.

_____ (1977), "Low Involvement in the Light of New Brain Research," paper presented at the AMA Attitude Research Conference (March 7), Las Vegas.

_____ (1978a), "The Two Brains: New Evidence," paper presented at the Advertising Research Foundation Annual Conference (October 16), New York.

_____ (1978b), "Toward an Ideal TV Pre-Test," paper presented at the AMA Advertising Research Conference (May 16), New York.

Siegel, B (1979), "TV's Effect from Alpha to Z-z-z," Los Angeles Times (March 11), pp. 1, 26.

Tolley, B. Stuart (1976), "Recent Use of the EEG in Newspaper Research," paper presented at the National Convention of the American Psychological Association (September 5), Washington, D. C.

Weinstein, Sidney (1978), "Brain Waves Determine the Degree of Positive Interest in TV Commercials and Print Ads," paper presented at the AMA 16th Annual Advertising Research Conference, "Physiological and Attitudinal Measures of Advertising Effectiveness," (May 16), New York.

_____ (1979a), "Brain Wave Analyses for Evaluation of TV Commercials and Print Ads Are No Longer Science Fiction," paper presented at the First Advertising Research Seminar of the Canadian Advertising Research Foundation (January 16), Toronto.

_____ (1979b), "Brain Wave Analyses for Evaluation of TV Commercials and Print Ads Are No Longer Science Fiction," Marketing Review, 34 (Feb./Mar.), 17-20.

_____ (1979c), "Brain Waves--Sound Waves: What Direct Measurement of Brain Activity Suggests About Exposure to Media," paper presented at the ANA/Radio Advertising Bureau Workshop (June 19), New York.

_____ (1979d), "Probing the Brain for Ad Input," Broadcasting (September 17), 22.

_____, Valentine Appel, and Curt Weinstein (1980), "Brain Activity Responses to Magazine and Television Advertising," Journal of Advertising Research, in press.

CHANGING VALUES AND LIFESTYLES

Arnold Mitchell, SRI International, Menlo Park

ABSTRACT

A nine-level typology of American consumers is outlined. The nine types are called Survivors, Sustainers, Belongers, Emulators, Achievers, I-Am-Me, Experiential, Societally Conscious, and Integrated. It is shown how these types fit together into a complex hierarchy. Forecasts of change on the groups are offered together with comments on some major social and market implications.

BACKGROUND

The research reported here is drawn from a three-year study of the values and lifestyles of adult Americans now in progress at SRI International. The program has about 70 corporate supporters. There are five program objectives:

1. Set forth a theory-based typology of values and lifestyles, including how they interrelate and how they influence the marketplace and the society.

2. Validate the typology by tieing it quantitatively to the real world. Quantification covers over 800 aspects of demographics, attitudes, regional distribution, activity patterns, and consumption patterns. Trends since 1973 have also been examined.

3. Project change in each lifestyle group for a decade ahead. Projections are offered under the conditions of four scenarios for the 1980s.

4. Show how the data and insights can be specifically applied in marketing, planning, product design, and numerous other areas.

5. Identify and comment on nonproprietary values research going on elsewhere.

THE TYPOLOGY

From the standpoint of the motivations underlying consumer spending, I think there are basically three different groups. These I call Money-Restricted, Outwardly Directed, and Inwardly Directed. Let me discuss each in turn.

Money-Restricted

We divide the Money-Restricted consumers into two groups called Survivors and Sustainers, but here I am combining them. These are households and individuals whose discretionary freedom in purchasing goods and services is severely restricted by lack of money. Hence, their buying is driven more by need than by choice. In general, these are the least psychologically free Americans and they are farthest removed from the cultural mainstream. Their demographics are well known. Purchases are dominated by survival and elemental security needs.

This kind of a consumer constitutes around 12% of the adult population today (that is, 18 million adults). This figure is estimated to drop to about 10% by 1990.

I have defined the second and third broad consumer groups in terms of David Riesman's celebrated dichotomy of "outer-directed" (or "other-directed") and "inner-directed"--but I should warn you that our use of these terms is very different from that of Riesman. This very distinction, I think, goes to the heart of why people buy as they do. Further, as we shall see, I think it represents a critical line separating yesterday's consumers from tomorrow's.

Outer-Directed

Outwardly directed consumers make up middle America. It is a tremendously diverse group. On the whole, such consumers buy with an eye to appearances and to what other people think. Since externals are so important, they tend to buy in accord with established norms--in fact, what they do establishes national norms. Our figures indicate that consumers motivated chiefly by outer-directed concerns today constitute 71% of Americans--that is, almost 110 million adults. I suggest there are three major types of outwardly directed consumers: Belongers, Emulators, and Achievers.

Belonger. The Belonger seeks to become part of the group
via his or her purchases. The prime drive is to fit in, not
stand out. Hence, this is a conforming, unexperimental kind of
person. Many live in the country, many in the aging frame
houses of small towns. These people tend to be puritanical,
formal, matriarchal, suspicious of the new, dutiful, following,
nostalgic, and sentimental. They are the heart of much family
buying. Although they participate in fads, they are not the
innovators: they join the fad in the third or fourth wave.
Income, education, and social status tend to be middle or less.
The group has about it an aura of old-fashionedness, reliability,
and dependability--like a tree with a deep taproot. There are
many who find this reassuring in a world of tumbling change.

About 38% of today's consumers are Belongers. This makes
them the largest single subgroup in our typology, numbering
close to 60 million adults. For reasons I won't go into, I
think the number of Belongers will shrink over time. Hence, I
place the fraction of Belonger buyers at around 33% ten years
from now.

Emulator. The Emulator is spectacularly--indeed flamboy-
antly--outer directed. He emulates the buying patterns of
those he considers more successful or richer than he. Such
consumers buy for status and material conspicuousness. They
put their money where it shows--on highly visible items such
as clothes, autos, and office furniture. The nouveau riche is
a standard stereotype. Male or female, they tend to be pretty
macho. These are people on the climb, highly concerned with
the impressions they make, and at the stage in life of high am-
bition and maximum social and job mobility.

Emulation buyers tend to be aggressive, ostentatious, ambitious, active, status-conscious, manipulative. These people
are often loud and blatant to cover up the uncertainty--in fact,
insecurity--inherent in the act of emulating rather than being
one's own self. Hence, they feverishly follow the current
vogue. Many Emulators have good incomes, often of recent vin-
tage.

Emulation buying appears to be a transition stage between
the Belonging and Achieving modes. As such, it will never be
as significant as the two more stable states on either side of
it. Such people make up about 10% of the population. We think
their numbers will slowly drop over time. In the past this has
been a heavily male group, but this seems to be changing as
large numbers of women move up career ladders. You'll also be
interested to know that blacks make up 23% of this ambitious,
powerfully upwardly mobile group. There is a fascinating story
here which I haven't time to go into.

Achiever. The Achiever is the driving and driven person, oriented to success, who commonly expends much of his or her wealth, activity, and energy on the good things of life. Achievers want the best and are willing to work hard for it. Work and the Puritan ethic are central to this consumer to the point that leisure, too, must be busy and productive. This is a rugged individualist in the frontier tradition--competitive, self-confident, and willing to try the new, especially if the newness smacks of technological innovation. At the same time, they don't want too much change because they're on top and really radical change might shake them off. The Achiever lives very much in a world designed to reflect his or her central drives. This means the home is a display place and the office is a symbol.

Most Achiever consumers are well educated. Their affluence enables them to support a large fraction of the high-profit luxury and gift markets. They are people of great influence in business, politics, and the professions. These people are the pace-setters for the Emulators and represent the "establishment" to social critics.

The Achievers are a gifted group having built today's enormously successful corporate system and market economy. And it is also largely their children who are creating the new waves of values. And, indeed, I am one of those who believes that the Achievers of 15 and 20 years from now will have adopted many of the so-called "new values" that I shall come to in a minute.

In terms of numbers Achievers today represent about 24% of the population, making them the second largest consumer group in our typology at over 35 million. My guess for ten years hence is 22%. This represents very little change in absolute numbers.

Inner-Directed

The third, and final, broad consumer type I have designated as inwardly directed consumers. As I hope the name implies, these people buy chiefly to meet their own inner wants and pleasures as opposed to responding primarily to the norms of others. To the extent these people form cliques, they create specialized mass markets, but the dominant feature of their buying is self-expressive diversity. We think this is the fastest-growing consumer category--indeed the only expanding segment of the three main types. We look for the number of Inner-Directeds to rise from about 17% of adult Americans to over 25% in the late 1980s.

We have divided the ranks of the Inner-Directed into four
types: I-Am-Me, Experiential, Societally Conscious, and Integrated. I'd like to touch on each.

I-Am-Me. The I-Am-Me consumer is narcissistic and fiercely
individualistic, insisting on buying what appeals to his or
her whim--and the whim is made of iron! They are emphatic on
buying things that are masculine or feminine, nostalgic or
avant-garde, funky or classic. The I-Am-Me style seems to be
strongly age-regulated, typifying relatively young people,
often single, relatively well-educated, and commonly still in
school or starting off in business or a profession. The mode
seems to be an early stage in the development of inwardly
oriented living still sharing many of the attributes of outer-
directedness. As such, it is a stage through which many pass
but few linger.

We think that no more than about 4% of consumers are I-Am-
Me types. For reasons I need not set forth, we do not expect
this percentage to change greatly in the decade to come.

Experiential. An important emerging life pattern, I think,
is that of the Experiential consumer. The Experiential consumer is a person who seeks direct experience, deep involvement, intense personal relationships, and a rich inner life.
The second-hand, the vicarious, the nonparticipative is ana-
thema. These kinds of people loom large in many of the avant-
garde movements; they are active in "far-out" ideas ranging
from astrology, to yoga, to transcendental meditation, to para-
psychology. Their desire for direct, often unusual, experience
leads them to such sports as hang-gliding, backpacking, and
water beds; to such home pursuits as baking, wine making, gar-
dening, and crafts; to such pastimes as meditation and study of
the occult; and to such activities as volunteer social work.
Strongly person-centered, such consumers tend to be well-
educated, somewhat intellectual, esthetically inclined, and
with good financial prospects. About 6% of today's consumers
are of this ilk--a percentage I think could almost double in
the next ten years as inward orientation becomes a more accepted and acceptable part of the national scene.

Societally Conscious. Another consumer segment probably
slated for major increases I have called the Societally Conscious consumer. This is a person acutely aware of societal
issues, imbued with a "spaceship earth" philosophy, and adamant
about living in a "socially responsible" way. Many are young,
but there is strong representation at all age levels. One expression of this life pattern is simple living or "voluntary
simplicity."

I think the Societally Conscious consumer may turn out to be the fastest growing group in the next ten years. Growth from 5 or 6% to perhaps 12% of the population is projected. This is at the extraordinary rate of 8 or 9% per year. It will come, I think, both from the push of events and the pull of what can be.

Integrated. The final consumer segment I call the Integrated consumer. By this, I mean consumers able to live in accord with an inner sense of what is fitting, self-fulfilling, releasing, and balanced. The image is of a fully mature person in a psychological sense, highly integrated in the various domains of life, and quite certain of what she or he likes. Such consumers are entirely free to try (or not try) anything that appeals. Self-actualizing, they tend to be indifferent to judgments of others. They swing easily in matters they consider inconsequential. In matters they consider important, however, they are likely to be strongly mission-oriented. Their global perspective makes them informed, ecologically alert consumers. Most such people are well-educated and many hold professional or managerial jobs and have good or excellent incomes.

People of this level of development are rare and no doubt will always be unusual. My guess is that only about 2 or 3% of today's consumers qualify as Integrated. My guess for 1988 is 5%. The living patterns established by this group are likely to set the standard for inner-oriented people, just as the style of Achievement consumers tend to form the template for Emulation-type buyers.

Summary of Projections

To summarize our projections: I look for a mild decline in the percentage of Money-Restricted and Outer-Directed people in the next decade and a whopping increase in the ranks of the Inner-Directeds. If the future unfolds as I anticipate, the number of Inner-Directed consumers will grow at around 6% per year and hence will come close to doubling in the coming decade. In the late 1980s there will be close to 20 million additional inner-directed adult consumers. About a fourth of the population will be espousing Inner-Directed values. But note, too, that the nation ten years from now will still be dominated by Outer-Directedness at a ratio of about 2-1/2 to 1. In other words, the gyroscope of tradition will still be spinning 10 and 15 years from now.

The Double Hierarchy

I unfortunately do not have time to discuss the theory underlying our scheme. But I would like to show how we have put our segments together. In the accompanying diagram the

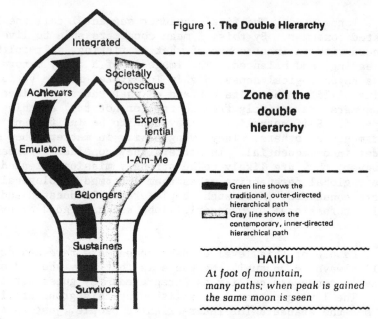

Figure 1. **The Double Hierarchy**

Integrated

Societally Conscious

Achievers

Experiential

Emulators

I-Am-Me

Belongers

Sustainers

Survivors

Zone of the double hierarchy

■ Green line shows the traditional, outer-directed hierarchical path

▨ Gray line shows the contemporary, inner-directed hierarchical path

HAIKU
At foot of mountain,
many paths; when peak is gained
the same moon is seen

darker arrow on the left portrays the outer-directed route to the top and the lighter arrow on the right the inner-directed route. What we call the "zone of the double hierarchy" is a hallmark of our times and a phenomenon that has not occurred before in history.

IMPLICATIONS

If you buy this way of looking at things, I believe a bit of thought will convince you that a lot of large and small implications can be deduced from our scheme. In our Values and Lifestyles Program at SRI, we have dealt in detail with many kinds of implications for broad social change, for markets and marketing, for planning, among others. Here I shall limit myself to a handful of the major implications bearing on business and society.

(1)   The marketplace will become even more <u>segmented</u> as Americans continue to move up both prongs of the hierarchy. Mass markets will split into specialized mass markets, and these will split into clique markets, and cliques will split into markets for the one-of-a-kind.

(2)   There will be <u>two elites</u> in products and services-- one serving the status needs of the Outer Directeds and the other the less visible drives of the Inner Directeds. The latter ask not what a product says <u>about</u> them but what it does <u>for</u> them. Theirs is the world of process over product.

(3)   For several reasons I think you will experience greater demand for the authentic, natural, and replaceable or recyclable. This means less plastic, more wood, wool, cotton; fewer replicas, more originals; more handmades, more imports, more uniques.

(4)   The war between the elites portends a period of much societal turbulence; our hope lies in bringing the insights of the Integrated person to the realms of less developed people. There is a book in that sentence.

(5)   The leading edge of values I would expect to shift in a variety of directions:

    ...from quantity toward quality
    ...from the group toward the individual
    ...from abundance toward sufficiency
    ...from formality toward flexibility
    ...from fads toward fashion
    ...from complexity toward simplicity
    ...from spendthrift toward frugality
    ...from waste toward conservation
    ...from secretiveness toward openness
    ...from tradition toward the experimental
    ...from the impressive toward the meaningful

(6)   Finally, I believe you will increasingly be working in a society more esthetically aware, more demanding of good taste, more open to the inventive than any society in the history of mankind. I look for a remarkable and thrilling renaissance in essentially every field of the arts as Experiential people move into their years of high creative productivity.

I'm saying that the world will be moving on in that funny way it has. I hope you will be there waiting for it.

"CRISIS" RESPONSE OF THE AMERICAN PUBLIC

Roy G. Stout, The Coca-Cola Company, Atlanta
Raymond H. Suh, The Coca-Cola Company, Atlanta

ABSTRACT

A number of studies were conducted in response to the negative publicity on soft drink products. Studies illustrated the conditioning of the American public to crisis after crisis in the '70's, and there is a great deal of stability in the thinking of the American public. With many issues publicized, one should be concerned, but one should not panic.

INTRODUCTION

Nearly all, if not all, consumer packaged goods companies have had to recall products because of quality control procedure breakdowns, or a change in governmental regulations. Such actions invariably have caused management a great deal of concern. What will happen to sales? What will happen to the consumer's image of the product— of the corporation? Will there be trouble with the trade? Will distribution be reduced? Over the years, the management of Coca-Cola USA have had occasion to deal with these "crisis" issues.

While it is a good healthy sign, for the good of the corporation, for management to have these concerns, usually the consumer is less excitable and less "fickle" than we think; and that is to our benefit. One hypothesis is, that in times of crisis, the American public does not get nearly as excited as we think they might; and what we may regard as a crisis, quite often, is ho-hum to the American consumer. Some of our past experiences are good illustrations of this point.

STUDY FINDINGS

A few years ago, Coca-Cola USA had in test market a carbonated flavored soft drink, containing real fruit juice, under the brand name Sugarbush. The product, in orange and grape flavors, was very heavily distributed in the test market city. A rather aggressive advertising campaign was in place to make the public aware of the new product. Something apparently went astray in our formulation for not very long after introduction the product began to ferment. The fermentation process caused an excessive build-up of pressure with the potential of exploding the containers. Once this became known, the company immediately began to recall the product; and within 24 hours, all product was removed from the shelves in all stores.

The company was also very concerned about any product that might be in home inventory; and within hours, a new TV commercial was produced explaining the problem. The public was advised that if they had any product with the Sugarbush label, they should treat it as potentially dangerous, wrap it in a towel and then dispose of it. This commercial was run at very high levels within 48 hours of the company's knowledge of the problem.

A few days later, a follow-up consumer survey was conducted to assess the damage that may have been done to the corporate image of the Coca-Cola. Much to the surprise of everyone, the public's overall attitude toward the company was improved because they were very appreciative of the speed, honesty, and integrity with which the company approached the problem. It was quite a relief to management that there was no damage to the brand image of Coca-Cola.

Another illustration occurred in May, 1976, when the Marketing Research Department was briefed on a story that a TV station, in a major U.S. city, planned to release on their 5 P.M. and 10 P.M. news shows.

Briefly, the news item reported a consumer claiming to have found a rat's foot in a bottle of Coca-Cola. Because she was so upset about the discovery, she called a local TV station. The station, looking for a newsworthy item, made a visit to the lady's house, filmed the story, and put it on the five o'clock news.

The Marketing Research Department was requested to conduct a telephone survey to obtain an estimate of the awareness levels of this news item and what effect the news item would have on the image of Coca-Cola. Interestingly enough in the same city, a week later, the same station reported on certain unsanitary production conditions in the local Pepsi-Cola bottling plant. A telephone survey was conducted one day after that story to determine the extent to which the consuming public was concerned.

A summary of these surveys indicates:

- 13% of those interviewed were aware of
  the news item pertaining to the foreign
  material found in a soft drink bottle.

- Of that 13% aware, 58% indicated that
  the brand was Coca-Cola, while 25% said
  it was Pepsi.

The second survey results, remember, concerning the unsanitary conditions reported in the Pepsi plant, are as
follows:

- 3.3% of the people interviewed recalled
  something about an unsanitary production
  facility.

- And of those that did remember, 40% said
  it was Coca-Cola and 40% said it was
  Pepsi-Cola.

In June, 1976, shortly after the introduction of
Coca-Cola in the 32-ounce plastic bottle in Connecticut, there
was a lot of concern in the Danbury area because of the
activities of the editor of the local newspaper. He was writing editorials pertaining to environmental issues associated
with the plastic bottle, implying among other things a possible link between plastic and cancer.

As a result of the publicity, a study was conducted on
July 1 and 2 when approximately 250 people were interviewed
in the Hartford area as a control group; and 250 were interviewed in the Danbury area as a test group.

When asked the question pertaining to likes of plastic
bottle,

- 78% from the Danbury area said they
  liked the plastic soft drink bottle
  a lot or liked it a little bit;

- While 79% of these in the Hartford
  area said they liked it a lot or a
  little bit -- no difference between
  the two areas.

A consumer survey had been conducted in both areas prior
to the publicity by the local editor. In both Danbury and
Hartford, 16% of the respondents reported that they definitely
would buy the plastic bottle. After the publicity, the consumer survey showed 16% from the Danbury area said they would
definitely buy the plastic bottle; and 18% from the Hartford
area said they definitely would buy it. Results of this survey were very helpful in preventing those chain stores, in

Danbury, from discontinuing the sale of the plastic bottle.

In February, 1977, the FDA declared its intent to ban the acrylonitrile plastic bottle. Since Coca-Cola was the only company using this package, we were concerned about consumer attitude toward Coca-Cola as a result of having a package banned due to potential health hazards.

A survey was conducted during the evening of February 21 in New York and the State of Michigan. Information from this survey indicated a high awareness of the banning of the package.

When consumers who were buying the plastic bottle were asked what they would buy in place of the plastic, 97% said they would buy other packages of Coca-Cola, again indicating no great consumer attitudinal change toward Coca-Cola as a result of a regulatory action.

On March 16, 1977, shortly after the FDA's announced intent to ban saccharin, a survey of approximately 500 users of low-calorie soft drinks was conducted.

In this survey there was an extremely high consumer interest. Ninety percent of the low-calorie soft drink users were aware five days after the announcement of the FDA's intent to ban saccharin. The FDA's planned intention, however, was not necessarily approved by the American public. In that survey it was found that only 6% of the sample thought, based on the evidence provided, that the FDA should ban saccharin. Approximately 32% said they thought it would be sufficient to put a warning statement on the container. Fifty-two percent indicated that they thought no further action should be taken until further research could be done and that such research should be done. Ten percent felt that no action should be taken.

This information is startlingly different than results of a survey conducted in October, 1969, after the cyclamate ban. In that survey, about 80% of those interviewed approved of the FDA action in 1969; while in 1977, 6% approved of it.

What you are seeing from 1969 to 1977 is the conditioning of the American public to crisis after crisis after crisis; and as a result, they are less inclined to be concerned about actions of a regulatory body.

CONCLUSION

In summary, these examples illustrate that there is a great deal of stability in the thinking of the American public. This, of course, does not say that you can ignore the loud voices of a few do-gooders. However, it does illustrate to you that with many issues with which you may be concerned, there may be only a small group of individuals involved, and while you should be concerned you shouldn't panic.

MEASURE EQUIVALENCE AND RELIABILITY DIFFERENTIALS: A SPECIAL PROGRAM FOR CROSS NATIONAL MARKETING RESEARCH

Harry L. Davis, University of Chicago, Chicago
Susan P. Douglas, New York University, New York
Alvin J. Silk, Massachusetts Institute of Technology, Boston

ABSTRACT

Multinational marketers must frequently undertake cross-national surveys in order to support decisions regarding marketing strategies. A commonly-overlooked threat to the validity of country-by-country comparisons is variation in the reliability of measurements due to various types of non-equivalencies of questionnaires. This paper explores the extent of this type of non-sampling error using data from a five country study. Significant between-sample reliability differentials were uncovered and systematic differences were uncovered and systematic differences were identified by question type but not by country or linguistic group. Procedures for identifying and correcting unreliability are briefly discussed.

BACKGROUND

A number of writers have inventoried the problems faced by multinational firms in attempting to operate simultaneously in several different countries. Buzzell (1968) cites differences across countries in customer needs, competition, and the structure of distribution as common barriers to a standardized marketing strategy. A recent empirical study of U.S. and European multinationals identifies deficiences in planning, marketing expertise at the subsidiary level, and the amount of information relating to local markets as sources of tension or conflict between the headquarter and subsidiary levels (Wiechmann and Pringle 1979).

A fundamental question that underlies many of these problems is the extent to which experience gained in one country can be used to guide marketing mix decisions in another country. Consider the following cases:

A European multinational concludes that it can achieve considerable production economies by standardizing the design of its line of small electrical appliances. A key issue, however, is the extent to which consumers in several different countries will accept the new line. A cross-national marketing research study is therefore undertaken.

61

A French dairy company decides to enter the North
American market with a line of expensive cheeses.
The Director of Advertising strongly advocates using
the same basic advertising appeal that had served
the company well in France for over twenty years.
The advertising agency argues, on the other hand,
that American motivations for buying and consuming
cheese are substantially different from the French
consumer. Research is carried out in several countries in order to resolve the controversy.

In both examples, the discovery of market differences provides
a justification for "localized" marketing strategies, while the
absence of any significant differences bolsters a case for
international standardization of marketing programs.

The purpose of this paper is to introduce and discuss one
additional problem confronting the multinational marketer.
Specifically, we consider the issue of whether the observed
similarities or differences in markets as revealed in data obtained from respondents residing in several locations are, in
fact, real. While this issue has rarely been addressed, particularly in the context of cross-national research, there are
strong a priori reasons to believe that the likelihood of
drawing invalid conclusions is indeed substantial when data are
being collected concurrently in several countries. In a related
context, Lipstein (1975a; 1975b; 1977) has warned market researchers that their preoccupation with sampling error is greatly
exaggerated given the magnitude of non-sampling error present
in survey results. He argues, moreover, that the common tactic
of increasing sample size in order to reduce sampling error may
actually be counterproductive since the complexities of administering large sample surveys are likely to introduce additional non-sampling error. The researcher carrying out a
cross-national study faces the difficult task of achieving both
linguistic and conceptual equivalence of questionnaire items
(Whiting 1968; Rao and Rao 1979; Angelmar and Pras 1978).
Sechrest, Fay, and Zaidi (1972) have identified several different
aspects of equivalence in transporting a survey from one country
to another including vocabulary, idiomatic, grammatical-
syntactical, experiential and conceptual. The problem of non-
sampling error would therefore seem to hold in spades for the
kinds of consumer studies that multinational companies must
undertake.

To the extent that the measuring instruments used in cross-
national research are unreliable, and particularly to the extent
that reliability levels vary across countries, the implications
are serious. As is well known, unreliability of observations
as a consequence of the presence of random measurement error

attenuates the precision of estimators and reduces the power of statistical tests of hypotheses (Cochran 1968). What might appear to be market-by-market differences between some predictor and criterion variable instead might reflect variations in the reliability of consumers' responses to questionnaire items or scales rather than any real differences.

DATA

The availability of data from a larger study of family decision making conducted in five countries provides an unusually rich opportunity to explore the presence of non-sampling error in cross-national research. Convenience samples of households in the U.S., Great Britain, France, Belgium, and Canada provided information on various constructs commonly used in consumer surveys. These included: (1) demographic and background characteristics, (2) self-reports of behavior in the form of ratings about involvement in household tasks and decisions, and (3) life-style/psychographic variables. The first two of these were measured on single item categorical scales while the life-style variables are composite scores based upon several items. An interesting feature of this study is the fact that self-administered questionnaires were completed independently by both the husband and the wife within each family. The questionnaire was originally developed in English and then translated into French. In order to deal with various linguistic differences, the initial French version of the questionnaire was modified by "local experts" to reflect the language usage habits in Belgium, France, and French Canada. Each version was then translated back into English and checked for consistency with the original. A detailed account of the study's method and results is reported in Davis, Douglas, and Silk (1980).

RELIABILITY ASSESSMENT

Reliability estimates for the demographic as well as for the decision and task involvement questions were obtained by cross-tabulating husbands' and wives' responses to the same item and then computing a measure of agreement between them. A coefficient proposed by Cohen (1960) and discussed in Bishop, Feinberg, and Holland (1975, pp. 395-397) and Kraemer (1978) was used. The measure (K) reflects the excess of observed over chance agreement, normalized by the maximum possible value of this difference, given the particular form of the marginal distribution observed for the two sets of responses. The coefficient is zero when the observed agreement is just equal to that expected by chance and unity when the maximum possible excess of observed over chance agreement is obtained. The re-

liability of the life style variables was assessed by means of
the Kuder-Richardson (Formula 20) coefficient (Guilford 1954,
pp. 380-383). Since each of the variables was a composite score
based upon adding together individual items that had loaded
heavily on an underlying factor, the question addressed is
simply whether the alternative lingustic versions of the
questionnaire have the same internal consistency properties.

FINDINGS

Two major findings emerge from these data. Both conclusions reinforce our earlier expectation of finding varying
reliability levels in cross-national studies of consumers and
the need for appropriate adjustments for unreliability.

1. The threat to validity due to unreliability of measurement is less for the "hard" variables such as demographic or
household characteristics than for the "soft" variables such
as task/decision involvement and life style/psychographic
factors.

A comparison of levels of husband-wife congruence for the
set of ten demographic and other more or less "invariant" household characteristics showed a high degree of reliability in all
five of the country samples.[1] All fifty (K) coefficients were
significantly different from zero; the percentage of couples
providing identical reports ranged from 85% to 95%. Relatively
few differences in classifying households on these variables
would therefore occur if one spouse supplied information rather
than the other. The overall level of reliability attained for
background characteristics will serve as a benchmark or standard
for comparing our results in the case of questions relating to
marital roles and life styles.

Considerably less agreement between husbands and wives was

_____

[1]The background characteristics included were (1) length
of marriage, (2) number of children, (3) husband's age, (4)
wife's age, (5) wife's employment, (6) husband's education,
(7) wife's education, (8) type of dwelling, (9) number of
applicances, and (10) total family income.

evident for the five task/decision items.[2] While the levels of
agreement exceeded those expected by chance, the K coefficients
were not high. In the case of the demographic characteristics,
more than half were greater than .9 whereas here only half
exceeded .5. The proportion of cases in which husbands and
wives gave identical reports of their relative involvement
varied from 62 to 89 per cent with most cases falling in the
70-75 percent range. Thus, a choice of which spouse to interview would obviously make a difference in how a significant
percentage of households would be classified.

The lowest levels of reliability were found in the measurement of life style variables.[3] The median value of the 30
Kuder-Richardson coefficients was not high--.504 and .533 for
wives and husbands respectively. Moreover, at 90 percent
confidence intervals, one of the wives' and three of the husbands'
coefficients were not significanlty different from zero.

   2. <u>There is no evidence of consistently high or low reliability for any individual country or language group</u>.

As part of the analysis of background characteristics, the
extent of association in the ranking of the K coefficients was
examined for the five countries across the ten variables. No
more consistency was uncovered than would be expected by chance.
Similarly, a handful of between sample differences was dis-
cernable for the five items regarding task and decision involvement but they were not concentrated within any particular
country or question. Variation in the reliability coefficients
for the life style items also did not relate in any obvious
way to country or language differences.

------

   [2] These included: (1) taking care of savings and invest-
ments, (2) making travel reservations, (3) going shopping for a
new car, (4) going to the supermarket, and (5) suggesting going
out for dinner. Respondents rated their involvement in each on
a three-point scale: "mainly husband," "joint or shared responsibility," and "mainly wife."

[3] The six variables are composite measures of individual
traits or value/personality orientations termed "orderliness,"
"anxiety and control," "traditionalism," "male dominance,"
"Task allocation," and "female role perception." A full
description of each can be found in Douglas and Wind (1978).

The fact that non-sampling error was present without any systematic pattern underlines the problems of drawing valid cross-national comparisons. If researchers fail to diagnose the presence and magnitude of unreliability and make the necessary adjustments, they run the risk of being mislead regarding cultural differences or similarities.

CONCLUSIONS

This paper began by citing the many problems faced by multinationals in carrying out cross-national surveys of consumer behavior. To this already long list of difficulties we have introduced another one, namely presence of non-sampling error. It has been shown that measure unreliability is present in the cross-national context particularly for attitudinal and the more subjective household information. The consequence of this form of error-in-the-variables is to attenuate the precision of estimators and reduce the power of statistical tests.

Just as researchers have grappled with other complexities of carrying out multi-nation surveys, a strategy for detecting and correcting unreliability in key measures must be put in place. There are several methodologies that are responsive to this important task. Internal consistency reliability statistics can be derived from the same study when a variable is measured by a multiple item scale. For the commonly-used single item measures, it is necessary to obtain reliability estimates in other ways, such as interviewing both husband and wife when relevant or by conducting special test-retest studies. There have also been significant developments in econometrics and psychometrices (Goldberger 1971; Griliches 1974) leading to formal statistical methods, including soft-ware packages, that take explicit account of this type of errors-in-variables problem.

All of these methodologies require that reliability estimates be made available routinely for cross-national surveys just as interviewer verification and reports of sampling errors have become standard operating procedures. The "invisibility" of unreliability when not specifically measured is a convenient way to avoid the problem but does not obviously eliminate or even reduce unreliability. The expense of carrying out the appropriate diagnostics and statistical corrections is also not a valid excuse. The cost of reliability assessment is insignificant when compared with the possible monetary loss of making a key strategic error based upon invalid research. All of this points to escalating the complexity of carrying out cross-national research, but then who ever said that multinational marketing was going to be easy?

REFERENCES

Angelmar, Reinhard and Bernard Pras (1978), "Verbal Rating
    Scales for Multinational Research," European Research, 6
    (March), 62-67.

Bishop, Yvonne M. M., Stephen E. Feinberg, and Paul W. Holland
    (1975), Discrete Multivariate Analysis, Cambridge, MA:
    M.I.T. Press.

Buzzell, Robert D. (1968), "Can You Standardize Multinational
    Marketing?" Harvard Business Review, 46 (November), 102-113.

Cochran, William G. (1968), "Errors of Measurement In
    Statistics," Technometrics, 10 (November), 637-666.

Cohen, Jacob (1960), "A Coefficient of Agreement for Nominal
    Scales," Educational and Psychological Measurement, 20
    (Spring), 37-46.

Davis, Harry L., Susan P. Douglas, and Alvin J. Silk (1980),
    "A Cross National Comparison of the Reliability of Selected
    Measurements from Consumer Surveys", Working Paper 1110-80,
    Sloan School of Management, Massachusetts Institute of
    Technology, April.

Douglas, Susan P. and Yoram Wind (1978), "Examining Family Role
    and Authority Patterns: Two Methodological Patterns,"
    Journal of Marriage and Family, 40 (February).

Goldberger, Arthur S. (1971), Econometrics and Psychometrics:
    A Survey of Commonalities," Psychometrika, 36 (June),
    83-107.

Griliches, Zvi (1974), "Errors in Variables and Other Inobser-
    vables," Econometrika, 42 (November), 971-998.

Guilford, J. P. (1954), Psychometric Methods, New York: Wiley.

Kraemer, Helene C. (1979), "Ramifications of a Population Model
    K as a Coefficient of Reliability," Psychometrika, 44
    (December), 461-472.

Lipstein, Benjamin (1975), "In Defense of Small Samples,"
    Journal of Advertising Research, 15 (February), 33-42.

_____(1975), "On the Limits of Reliability in Social and Commercial Surveys," Proceedings, ESOMAR Conference on Quality in Research, European Society for Opinion and Marketing Research, Amsterdam, 17-39.

_____(1977), "Are You Paying More and Getting Less?" Proceedings, 23rd Annual Conference, Advertising Research Foundation, New York, 59-62.

Rao, Prakasa V. V., and Nandini V. Rao (1979), "An Evaluation of the Bardis Familism Scale in India," Journal of Marriage and the Family, 41 (May), 417-421.

Sechrest, Lee, Todd L. Fay and S. M. Hafeez Zaidi (1972), "Problems of Translation in Cross-Cultural Research," Journal of Cross-Cultural Research, 3 (March), 41-56.

Whiting, W. M. John (1968), "Methods and Problems of Cross-Cultural Research," in G. Linzey and E. Aronson, eds., The Handbook of Social Psychology, Volume 2, 2nd edition, Reading, Mass.: Addison-Wesley, 693-728.

Wiechmann, Ulrich and Lewis G. Pringle (1979), "Problems that Plague Multinational Marketers," Harvard Business Review, 57 (July-August), 118-124.

DEMOGRAPHICS THAT WILL SHAPE THE NEXT DECADE

Vincent P. Barabba,
Bureau of the Census,
U.S. Department of Commerce, Washington, D.C.

ABSTRACT

Several major trends took place in American society during the 1970's that reflect our changing
lifestyles and values. This presentation explores
these .trends -- some of them as dramatic as any in
our history -- and where they may lead in the current
decade.

I'm happy to be here with you today for a number
of reasons. For one, I know you and the organizations you represent are deeply concerned with trends
revealed by the Census Bureau's demographic data. So
I'm especially pleased to share with you the more important trends of the 1970's, because they will play
a major role in shaping the destiny of the Nation in
the years ahead.

I'm also glad to be here, not only because I
represent the Federal Government, but also because I
share with you the concerns of private industry and
marketing research. I have in the past directed my
own research company and early next year I will return to my regular post as market research director
for a major corporation which will go nameless. But,
if you want a copy of this talk I'll be happy to send
you one.

I have yet another reason for wanting to talk to
you today. We are about to take the most important
decennial census in our history, and you can help us
get the most complete and reliable data ever produced
from a census. I ask that you lend your support to
the effort, both within the research community and in
the communities where you live. We will be happy to
furnish you and your organizations--immediately--with
ample materials to help sell the census. We also
will be glad to send you a schedule that tells you
when the results of the census will be available for
your use.

Now that we know why I'm happy to be here let's
talk about the major trends that have taken place in
our society since the last census in 1970. Many of
them are quite important to you, since they reflect
changing lifestyles and values. Where possible we
will look at the 1980's and examine changes that contrast with the 1970's. Please remember, as I go
along, that the 1980 census will produce the same
type data on the local level, where most market decisions are actually made.

Let me start by saying that the 1970's have produced some of the most interesting and dramatic demographic trends of any decade in our history, and the
1980's promise to be no less interesting. One of the
most important is the rapidly changing age structure
of the population, particularly the maturing of the
post World War Two baby boom population. This is of
particular importance to you since there is an abun-
dance of evidence that different age groups have different attitudes. Also important is the impact of
changing patterns in marriage, divorce, and family
formation, as well as in the composition of the labor
force and the role of women in America. And finally,
we have seen major changes in where we live--changes
in movement both within and outside the metropolitan
areas, and from one part of the Nation to another.

We expect in this census to count some 222 million people, which will be a 9 percent gain over
1970. It is important to note that this will be one
of the smallest percentage 10-year increases in our
history. For instance, our gain from 1960 to 1970
was 13 percent. From 1950 to 1960 it was 19 percent.
And from 1940 to 1950, despite the War, it was 15
percent.

But at the same time, we have seen great numbers
of people added to the population, and this will continue. For instance, we added 24 million between
1960 and 1970, another 17 million in this past decade, and if present trends continue we should see
21 million more by the end of the 1980's. This is
more people than the combined current population of
about one-third of our states.

There have been some very striking contrasts,
with major political implications, in the regional
growth patterns in the last few years. The population continues to move westward and with it the West

70

experienced the largest regional increase--18 percent
from 1970 to 1979. The South also had a substantial
gain of 14 percent, but in the other two regions the
situation has been different. The North Central region grew by only 3 percent, while the Northeast did
not grow at all. Ordinarily one might consider this
bad news, but at least in the case of the relatively
crowded Northeast, the lack of growth may well carry
its own ecological and psychological blessings. The
economic concerns of no growth or poor growth, of
course, are another matter. And, of course, there
will be changes in political representation among the
regions.

Every region of the Nation experienced a natural
increase in its population in the 1970's, as the number of births exceeded the number of deaths. However, these natural increases were offset to a considerable extent by outmigration losses in the North
Central and Northeastern regions which have been
quite marked. For instance each of the two regions
lost nearly 700,000 people in just the years 1975
through 1978. In contrast, the South had a net in-
migration of a million people and the West, a total
of nearly 400,000.

We all know that the so-called sunbelt states
have been growing at a phenomenal rate, particularly
the states of Nevada, Arizona, Florida, New Mexico,
Texas, and Hawaii. Outside the sunbelt, the faster
growers have been Wyoming, Alaska, Utah, Idaho, and
Colorado. Obviously the smaller states have the
highest growth rates, but California will remain as
the most populous state. New York will remain second, and Texas will replace Pennsylvania as the third
largest.

The census is required by the U.S. Constitution
for reapportioning the seats in the House of Representatives and here we should see some changes among
the states based on the 1980 census results.

If the Bureau's trial reapportionment of the
estimated 1979 population holds true, three seats
would be gained by Florida and two each by Texas and
California. One seat would be gained by another
seven states--Arizona, Colorado, New Mexico, Oregon,
Tennessee, Utah and Washington. New York would lose
four seats and two seats would be lost by Illinois,
Ohio, and Pennsylvania. And finally four states

would lose one seat each--Massachusetts, Michigan, New Jersey, and South Dakota.

I should caution you, however, that even small shifts in the population can affect the gains and losses. For example in 1970 the 435th seat in the House was decided on a difference of fewer than 250 people.

Down below the state level we have noted a major reversal of past patterns of population growth. For the first time in our history, the metropolitan areas are growing less rapidly than the nonmetropolitan parts of the country. In fact, some of our largest metropolitan areas actually are losing population, and within them, the central cities in particular as a group are losing people.

Overall, the Nation grew by 8 percent from 1970 to 1979, but it's interesting to note that the metropolitan areas grew by only 6 percent compared with 12 percent in the nonmetropolitan areas. The central cities themselves experienced an actual population loss of 4 percent. And while the suburbs also grew by 15 percent, that is less than the rate of increase in the 1960's.

One of the more important demographic observations regarding our suburbs is the fact that since 1970, there has been an increase of 46 percent in the number of blacks who are suburbanites. This is a growth rate that far overshadows the black growth rate in any other geographic area, and suburban blacks now represent 20 percent of all blacks instead of the 16 percent that we noted back in 1970.

These recent shifts in the population that I have just mentioned will have a major influence on the social, economic, and political structure of the United States. For instance, many of us have for some time now considered that the day would come when migration would reduce the rural population to such a low level that the volume and rate of movement to the metropolitan centers would decline. But no one predicted that this would happen as soon as it has. I can in fact report that today, more people are moving from our large metropolitan areas than are moving to them, and all of these population shifts may be reflected in shifts in consumer attitudes as well, to the extent that the needs and desires of the

72

metropolitan and nonmetropolitan areas differ.

These patterns have caused regional population
shifts, and in this regard we can expect the most
impressive rate of movement to be to the sunbelt
states in the 1980's. Specifically I refer to the
belt of states that extends from Virginia through
Texas and on to Southern California.

What will happen after 1990 is more a matter of
speculation. But by that time, we are likely to have
seen fundamental changes in the national economic and
political power patterns of the Nation, primarily at
the expense of the Northeastern part of the country.
For example, the migration into the South that I
mentioned has included many professionals, educators,
managers and other executives who have accompanied
the move of some of the larger national organizations. Also, greater numbers of retirees have been
moving to the South in this decade, carrying their
own political and social convictions.

A major contributory factor in these regional
and other population shifts is that circumstances
have changed in recent years, so that people can
choose where they live on an entirely different basis
than previously. These include two important developments: rising income levels for some segments
of the population and decreasing family size. These
two factors are permitting people to place greater
emphasis on living conditions related to climate,
recreation, and compatible neighbors. All this has
its impact on the political styles of elected officials, and on other considerations, such as planning by business and industry, and a variety of
quantitative and qualitative shifts in values and
attitudes.

I would advise those in marketing research, as
well as officials at all levels of government, to
consider a number of other social and economic developments that we have noted since 1970, trends
that are likely to continue into the 1980's. I refer
to the formation of families and households, as well
as the changing age structure, and trends that have
been taking place in the labor force. What has been
happening in each of these areas is of major importance because together the changes are rapidly re-
weaving the social and economic fabric of our society.

First, changes in the makeup of households in this country since 1970 constitute one of the most intriguing phenomenons in recent times. We have seen a spectacular rise of 26 percent in the number of households from 1970 to 1980, and in this year's census we expect to count a total of about 80 million occupied households. This 26 percent increase over 10 years in the number of households is even more remarkable when one remembers that the population will have increased by only 9 percent during the same period of time. Looking further ahead, we estimate that by the year 1990, we should see 97 million households in the United States. Again another demographic change likely to raise sampling costs.

What we have observed here since 1970 is a dramatic increase in the number of persons living alone, which has helped reduce the average household size from 3.14 persons in 1970 to 2.78 persons in 1979, and possibly below the 2.50 level in 1990, if current trends continue. We have also noted a surge in nonfamily households totaling 66 percent since 1970 so that one out of every four households now consists of a person living alone or with non-relatives, and possibly one out of three in 1990. As part of this, we expect that by this year about five and a half million women 65 and over will be living alone, compared with only a million and a half men in that age category.

Another reason why the number of small non-family households has increased recently is because more young women are remaining single longer. For example in 1970 about one-third of the women aged 20 to 24 were unmarried but this year we expect this figure to be close to one-half. This is a major change, with sweeping ramifications.

Families, of course, are one type of household and we see two notable trends in regard to them. First, husband and wife families are growing at a much slower rate than the total of all households-- an increase of only 7 percent since 1970. Second, we have seen a rapid increase in the number of families maintained by women who have no husband present in the home. These families have increased by 50 percent in just the last nine years.

One should note that the family household is still by far the dominant type of household. But at

the same time, we should also note that the proportion of households maintained by a married couple is
declining. For example, in 1970 married couples comprised 70 percent of all households. At present,
their proportion has dropped to just over 60 percent.
And by the year 1990, we are likely to see a drop to
55 percent if present trends continue.

Each of these several trends on households has
had, and will continue to have, a tremendous impact
on planning at all levels, and these trends will
also have an impact on attitude studies. And at
least as strong an impact is being felt by changes
in the age structure of our society. The census will
highlight and document the widespread effect of
these changes. I think we should take a close look
at this age structure in light of its importance in
your own research. We are seeing some rapid changes
in this area because of changes in the annual number
of births in recent years.

When we look at the population under 5 years
old, we note fewer preschoolers in 1980 compared
with 1970, but we can expect more by the end of this
decade. We might reasonably expect a jump of 21 percent in this particular population between 1980 and
1990, to a total of 19 million. This is because of
the increasing number of women in the childbearing
years, who will be numerous enough to more than offset declining fertility rates. We hesitate to attempt a precise measure of the number of births in
the next 10 years because it requires making some
assumptions that might not hold up. But even the
lowest fertility projections by the Census Bureau
show an increase in the number of children under 5
by the year 1990.

Moving to the next age group, those 5 to 13
years old, we note that their number decreased during the 1970's, dropping from 37 million to an expected 30 million this year. This will be a 19 percent decrease in this age group, and we have seen
the effects in the closing of some elementary schools
and consolidation of others. But we do expect a
reversal of this trend between 1980 and 1990, when
we project an increase of about 3 million.

The number of adolescents of high school age
will be at about the same level this year as it was
in 1970--about 16 million. But between 1980 and 1990

we expect a decrease in these 14 to 17 year olds amounting to about 3 million, or 19 percent. Therefore the declines in elementary school enrollment that we have experienced in the 1970's will shift to the high schools in the 1980's.

We also expect a decline in the number of young adults between 1980 and 1990 of about 15 percent, which will amount to a loss of more than 4 million, or down to a total of about 25 million. This group, ages 18 to 24, increased in the past decade by about 19 percent, or by 5 million.

The age group that grew the fastest during the 1970's is that consisting of persons who are from 25 to 34 years old. This group increased by a very substantial 43 percent, or 11 million, between 1970 and 1980. During the 1980's this group will still be the fastest growing group, but will obviously become the 35 or 44 year old group as the decade unfolds. They are expected to grow by 42 percent, or 11 million.

The entire age bracket from 25 to 44 years old is particularly important to the U.S. economy because they represent the years when families are formed, homes are purchased, and careers are fashioned.

As each of these age groups changes in the decade ahead, fresh challenges will face the Nation, so I would like to summarize quickly what you can expect in the coming decade. First, the number of children under 5 is expected to increase, as well as those 5 to 13 years old. However, those of high school age will decrease in number, as well as those of college age. And the largest increase between 1980 and 1990 will take place among those 35 to 44 years old.

Finally, we have one other fast-growing population group, and I refer to those who are 65 years old and older. Their numbers grew by 5 million in the 1970's, and we can expect them to add another 5 million by the end of this decade. These figures convert to a gain of nearly 25 percent in the 1970's and another 20 percent in the 1980's.

Another important aspect of our society to look at quickly is the work force. The census also will most likely document on a local basis the labor

76

force trends that we have observed on the national level during the 1970's. This year's census should for instance show that we have a much younger labor force, and one in which half of all working-age women, as well as 50 percent of wives, are participating. Back in 1970 only about 40 percent of all women worked, the same percentage holding true for working wives. And projections indicate that around 60 percent will be in the labor force by 1990. Most noteworthy--at least from the standpoint of child care--is the 17 percentage point increase in labor force participation by women who are 25 to 34 years old, because most of them have young children.

The 1980 census also should document locally the effects of strong competition for jobs among the baby boom population. Among young people, blacks and Hispanics are having an especially difficult time finding their way into the economic mainstream. Fortunately, this problem will ease somewhat as we move through the next decade since we will see the effects of lower birth rates in recent years. On the other hand, it will pose other problems for business because the incoming labor pool will be smaller.

These are some of the trends that we will document next year in tens of thousands of communities across the country. I've covered a lot of ground, but it is important to convey what to expect from the coming census, and how the demographic and socioeconomic happenings of the '70's are sizing up for the 1980's.

I'd like to close the formal part of this talk by saying that I hope you will take every opportunity to use the forthcoming census data because I know that the changing trends and lifestyles revealed by the census will be of major importance in attitude research. And finally, since the census will provide such vitally needed data, I want to again ask for your support in our census activities.

WHY ATTITUDES PREDICT BEHAVIOR BETTER THAN
BEHAVIOR PREDICTS ATTITUDES

Harry E. Heller, Harry Heller Research Corp., Port Washington

ABSTRACT

Market Research still relies on behavioral measures as the criterion of market performance. But behavior measures are confused by marketplace conditions and tell us what happened in the past, not what will happen in the future. This paper suggests that we should be measuring "Attitude share of market" -- a more future oriented criterion of the performance of consumer products.

One would have to have been locked in a sound proof room located in a cave below the earth is surface to have avoided hearing the futurists and prognosticators talking about the impact of the 70's and making predictions (mostly dire) about what the 1980's will bring to us. This 10 year review is a consequence of our decimal numbering system providing experts with convenient points of time at which they can review what has been done in the past and venture a guess about what will be happening in the future.

The field of marketing and public opinion research has also had its share of predictions. Most of the ones I've read about deal with the impact of new technologies on the way we will be doing research. We've heard about cathode-ray interviewing, universal product code data collection, interactive TV opinion taking, and other advanced technologies providing instant information to waiting marketers. I am distressed, however, that all of these advances seem to be based upon new technologies and machines and few have called into question the very assumptions behind a need for quick behavioral data -- what these technologies measure best of all.

I see the 1980's as being much like the 1970's, and I see some trends that were established in the 1970's continuing. As an attitude researcher, I am worried by what I see. What concerns me is the continuing dependance, among those who use market research, on measures of behavior as the primary criterion of how they are doing in the marketplace. While Universal Product Code systems provide quick information of the effect of various marketing alternatives, it is a behavioral measure. Cathode-ray tube interviewing and interactive TV in the marketing research field is best used for questions that can be answered with a simple behavior report, yes-no, will-will not, etc.

Why am I "down" so much on behavior measures? Because we attitude researchers have let ourselves accept the belief that behavior should be the measure we predict; that behavior is the criterion against which to validate our attitude measures. That comes to the subject of this paper. After spending 20 years in this field in various capacities, I am convinced that two simple principles must guide our field.

1. The work of marketing research must be futuristic.

2. We can change market performance by properly under-standing attitudes behind the decision to purchase a product.

Unfortunately, behavior measures are a result of what went on before them observing behavior as a way of determining what's going on in the marketplace is not as good as measuring attitudes. Indeed, I am firmly convinced that attitudes are a better predictor of behavior than behavior is a predictor of the attitude of a person. I will demonstrate this by way of a story.

Several months ago at a restaurant with my daughter, we both ordered a steak and baked potato. When our plates arrived at our table, both of us took the baked potato, removed it from the plate and put it on the bread and butter dish. We smiled at each other when we noticed that the two of us had just carried out an identical behavior, and decided to exchange the attitude behind our behavior. My daughter felt the plate was not large enough to hold the steak and the baked potato to-gether without one or the other falling off at sometime during the meal. She removed it to the bread and butter dish to make room. I did it to separate the various courses of the meal so that they wouldn't be mixed together with a hodgepodge of tastes. I removed it to the bread and butter dish to keep it separate. Both of us carried out exactly the same behavior for completely different reasons.

Now let's say it was our job as marketers to encourage people to remove baked potatoes from dinner plates. By observ-ing and reporting our dinner time behavior, we would have determined the characteristics of those people who remove baked potatoes from dinner plates very well. It would have improved our media efficiency but told us very little about what can motivate people to remove their potatoes. However, knowing the attitudes, the underlying reasons behind the behavior, we would have done a superior way of affecting future behavior. If we found that a majority of people removed potatoes to make room, then the communication should deal with the size of the plate. If those who remove it to make room are younger, and those who do it to keep it separate are older, we would know what to say to whom. In terms of the things we are paid to do, future influence of market performance, attitude is a far better predictor of what to do than behavior.

If you feel that this is a trivial example, let me tell you about an attitude study I conducted 15 years ago. The study was conducted for a major manufacturer of bourbon, Old Crow. At the time we conducted the study, Old Crow was the largest selling bourbon in the United States and the second leading brand of all distilled liquors in the country. By every behavior measure, it was a successful product. We conducted an attitudinal study about the brand and found that Old Crow had serious attitude problems. The people who thought highly of Old Crow were older. The attitudes of newer customers coming into the category was that Old Crow is a product for older people and of lower quality and price. Another brand of bourbon, in fourth place in the category at the time, Jim Beam, looked like it had all of the positive images that these new users wanted. Yet, there were so few Jim Beam users at the time at which we did our study that Jim Beam, even with its positive images was found in fourth place. The entire bourbon category, too, was having attitude problems. We saw indications that consumer attitudes were moving toward lighter brands of distilled spirits. In this study conducted 15 years ago, we concluded three things:

1. Old Crow was in trouble, it would face shrinking acceptance among new bourbon users.

2. Among new users of bourbon, Jim Beam looked promising, it seems to be offering young bourbon users the kinds of images and characteristics that they are looking for.

3. The entire bourbon category appeared to be in bad trouble and would lose out to lighter spirits such as vodka and rum.

This study was conducted in an era when behavioral measures were used ahead of attitude measures. The results of the study were noted but made secondary to the strong behavioral data emerging from other studies. Fifteen years later what we predicted actually happened. As reported by Advertising Age recently, <u>Old</u> <u>Crow</u> is a minor brand in the category, <u>Jim</u> <u>Beam</u> has become the number one brand, and the entire bourbon category has shrunk in volume at the expense of vodka and rum.

Any company that bases its marketing intelligence on SAMI, Nielson and other market behavior measures will miss the boat in identifying the problems it faces in the future and how to overcome them.

If the story I just told sounds like ancient history, let me share with you some current attitude data that will tell us what is going to happen in the next few years. First, let us look at the behavioral data. We have recently conducted a national study among 1800 families for a major food company and asked respondents about their use of a large number of food products. One of the questions that we asked was to report to us their usage of main course alternatives. Here are the results of this question for three types of main course foods.

	Used 1-3 Times In The Past Week
Beef	91%
Chicken	66
Fish	37

From the results we would conclude that beef is used by 1/3 more consumers than chicken and by almost 2½ more consumers than fish.

We also asked our respondents an attitudinal question -- asking them to project their use of beef, chicken, and fish to the future. This table summarizes the result of that question.

WILL BE USED IN THE FUTURE

	More	Less	About The Same
Beef	4%	(17)	79
Chicken	(21%)	1	78
Fish	(27%)	2	71

Our conclusion is quite different when we look at attitudes:

Beef will become a shrinking category at the expense of chicken and fish.

81

Now we can obtain this kind of information behaviorly, but let us think for a moment about how difficult it would be. Shrinking markets are usually identified by tracking the performance of a brand or a product through a behavioral measure over time. If we used a syndicated service that reports the results of its audit every 2 months, it would probably take about six months to be able to identify a trend, i.e., 3 consecutive reductions in the level of use of the product.

If the issue were really critical we might let the tracking go on for another two months to make sure that this trend is really true. It would take between 6 and 9 months to identify a behavioral trend in the marketplace.

Yet, this trend can be identified by attitude research in a single study with the results analyzed at a single point in time. To show you real data, the U.S. Department of Agriculture, has been tracking the trends in per capita consumption of the same 3 foods we've been looking at.

PER CAPITA CONSUMPTION OF FOODS
(In lbs.)

	1969	1979	Change In lbs.
Beef & Veal	84.7	81.3	- 3.4
Poultry	46.7	62.0	+ 15.3
Fish	11.2	13.7	+ 2.5

How long would it have taken us to identify these 10 year trends on a yearly basis?

Beef consumption averaged a .34 lb. per year change, poultry a 1½ lb. per year change and fish a 1/4 lb. per year change. All of these changes would have been assumed to be random variations due to sampling. It would have taken us at least 2 to 5 years to really spot a trend. This trend was identified in a single interview in an attitude study.

This is not the only problem. Once a behavioral trend is established in a tracking study, there is no guarantee that we will have identified the underlying reasons for this trend. The reduction in the use of beef, for example, can be due to problems in price, a greater concern for cholesterol and fat, or an article in the newspaper linking by-products of barbecuing beef with cancer. The steps needed to arrest this trend would be unknown until we found out what the underlying reason for the change in behavior is. In contrast, from other attitudinal data in this study, we have identified clearly and easily the

82

reasons for the change in beef consumption. My client, the study sponsor, can take immediate steps by understanding what is going on.

Why does our industry pay so much attention to behavioral measures and force attitude measures to meet the validity requirement of the behavioral measures? Part of it, I feel, is due to the distrust or lack of understanding of attitude measures by non-researchers. Few practitioners, product managers and presidents realize that over the past decade, attitude measurement in our field has taken giant strides which makes it more useful, reliable, and predictive than the behavior measures.

So let me state now, for our collective clients -- the non-researchers who use our research ---

1. If you want to control and affect the future, you must measure the "attitude share of market" of your product, rather than the "share of market" it had several months ago. Right now, the preponderance of research budgets are weighted toward looking backward.

2. We researchers have the skills and techniques developed and in place, to tell you what aspects of your product you must change -- whether it be beliefs, benefits or images, to increase its "attitude share."

Much of this progress is due to several new developments in our field -- consumer decision theory, disaggregate data analysis, and other models that take what is inside each person's head to make a probability estimate of the person's brand behavior and then examines the data person by person -- to predict total market performance.

To understand how these developments come together, let us review an example of how to obtain attitude share of market.

Think of any category of products you yourself would buy - say beer. There are some beers you are not aware of, the unaware brands. Some you are aware of but know nothing about, the don't know brands; others you are aware of but refuse to buy, the rejected brands, and finally, there are those you are aware of and would consider buying. All of these groups have significance to the marketer. But, it is the final group of brands, those you are aware of and would considering buying that is critical. This group has been defined by various names in the literature. Some researchers call this group the "evoked set," or "brand set" or a term we prefer -- the "consideration frame." It best describes that frame of brands that people consider in making a product class decision.

For some people, this "set" may be only one product (a brand loyal person). For others, it may be three or four products. In the consumer product classes we have studied, the average number of products considered is between 3 and 5. The range (which depends upon the size of the competitive array) is from 1 to 38 products in our studies.

Each brand in this group has a unique probability of being purchased by each individual. If we were to determine each person's probability of buying each brand, and then aggregate over the entire sample, we would have a "snap-shot" of the market share of each product. We have done 30 such studies in product classes as diverse as paper cups, dinnerware and deodorants. When looked at closely, most analysts we work with agree that we are tapping something very close to market share. We call this "attitude share of market."

Just what is "attitude share of market"? And what isn't it?

First, we do not believe that any attitude system can reproduce the measure commonly called market share. The sample used may not have been randomly drawn. Market share is different in New York than in Cincinnati, on the West Coast or on the East Coast, in New Jersey and in New Orleans. In each market, a different brand array is present, priced differently, with different promotional activities, etc. New brands have unique repeat purchase functions which can increase or decrease market share and different degrees of distribution and out of stock exist. So "attitude share of market" is the share of business consumers would give your brand up to the point of purchase given the competitive array used in the study. This share is a function of the effectiveness of your advertising, the images held about your product and the competitive array. All other intermediate factors are due to non-attitude areas; distribution, sales force, etc. In product classes in which array, pricing, distribution, repeat purchase and other variables are about equal, we have found that "attitude share of market" validates the real market share that will be reported 3 months from now.

Now, if attitude share of market tells us what is going on in the minds of consumers now, how can we understand what to do to increase attitude share? To do this we must understand what underlies brand choice.

Let us go back to the individual consumer level. If each person has a unique brand array that is considered (consideration frame), and if each person has a unique probability of selecting each brand which when aggregated gives us attitude share of market, then the purpose of our marketing efforts should be to:

1. Move a brand into the consumer's consideration frame.

2. Once in the consideration frame increase the purchase probability of the brand relative to other brands in the frame.

We have found that the best way of increasing purchase probability is by increasing "choice" probability. If a person has more than one brand in the consideration frame, the brand that delivers more of what is considered important will have a higher probability of purchase. This model is based upon multi-attribute theory of Martin Fishbein.

In multi-attribute theory, if we know what attributes and benefits people consider important, and if we know what each brand delivers to them, we can determine the underlying reasons for choice of each of the brands in the competitive array.

By measuring importance of product attributes and "brand delivery" of attributes for the Fishbein brand choice model, we retain much of the market definition capability and data processing we have always had involving attitude segmentation and brand mapping.

I will state, unequivocally, that the studies we have conducted measuring "attitude share of market" were more useful and predictive to future strategy development than the behavioral studies traditionally conducted as a thermometer of brand performance.

As sure as I am that attitude measures are a better way of understanding and changing future market performance -- you can also be sure that our collective clients, the brand managers, marketing directors and corporate presidents, will want to hold onto behavioral measures to measure their markets. They do so because in the past we have failed to provide them with attitude data and meaning that is analogous to the data upon which they must make their financial decisions. As I have shown you here, today, that is not so any longer.

So I say, that the message of the 1980's should not be that there are machines, computers, and black boxes in research, but that we attitude researchers have finally developed measures about how people think about brands that are better predictors of what will be than traditional backward looking behavior measures, such as "market share," etc. This then is our charge. To communicate this revolution to our managers. Will you join me in this effort?

THEORIES OF ADVERTISING AND MEASUREMENT SYSTEMS

Benjamin Lipstein
Graduate School of Business Administration
New York University, New York

ABSTRACT

The more important theories of advertising are reviewed
and related to the more widely used systems of advertising
measurement based upon the number of exposures to the advertisement. Two omissions in current measurement systems are
discussed, dimensional response of advertising and miscomprehension of copy content.

INTRODUCTION

Implicitly, every attempt at measuring the effect of an
advertisement or commercial implies some theory of how advertising works. Theory is a useful device for suggesting an
explanation of how the world works and a valuable discipline
for relating these measurements to the world about us. There
are a number of criteria which are valuable in judging the
merits of a theory. A useful and effective theory of how
advertising works should fulfill most if not all of the following criteria:

1. It should be a reasonable representation of the
real world.
2. It should not be overly complicated, to facilitate
its application.
3. It should provide a basis for measurement.
4. It should provide insights about the process of
advertising which were not previously evident.
5. In its application, it should provide a basis for
prediction of the process under study.

The purpose of the paper is twofold. First, is to examine
the more widely considered theories of advertising and to
relate the various stages of the theories to current measurement practice. In the second part of the paper, a number of
new measurements are examined which have not become part of the
routine for evaluating viewer response to advertising.

At the outset, it seems advisable to classify the varieties of theories of advertising and narrow the range of the
discussion. In a very broad sense, we can identify four separate
areas of inquiry:

1.   Theories of how viewers see and respond to advertising.   These theories consider the various phases of
exposure and how viewers interact with the content of the
adverting and their reaction to the advertising campaign.

2.   Studies directed primarily at estimating the effect
of advertising. This effort has been of both an empirical
and theoretical nature and is exemplified by the
distributed lag models, the use of experimental designs
in estimating the effect of advertising and other multivariate methods of analysis.

3.   There is a class of work directed at the strategy of
advertising budget allocation. These efforts have been
directed at maximizing the efficiency of advertising
expenditures in achieving particular marketing goals.

4.   Finally, there is the very large area of consumer
behavior theory which encompasses theories of advertising
as well as other elements in the marketing process,
consumer reactions to environmental influences and consumer decision processes.

This discussion is directed at the first area, theories of
advertising which consider viewer exposure to advertising and
their reaction to the advertising.

THEORIES OF ADVERTISING

Theories of how advertising works appear to have formally
first appeared with Daniel Starch's early work in the nineteen
twenties. Other practitioners added to the realm of theory over
the ensuing years. However, with the growing interest in
advertising, the last twenty five years has seen an outflow of
a wide range of theories of how advertising works. Even for
the active practitioner of advertising, the great varieties of
theories of how advertising works and how consumers respond to
advertising, represents a confusing array of ideas.

Some meaningful classificaton of these theories is useful
to facilitate the positioning of theories to determine their
role in the development and evaluation of advertising, to aid
in the comparison of the ideas, to identify areas of conflict
nd hopefully to identify important omissions in these theoretical notions. The most common classification scheme for
comparing theories of advertising is the hierarchy-of-effects
classification. Lavidge and Steiner's (1961) work on the
hierarchy-of-effects of advertising have stood the test of time

well. Other reviewers of the field like Michael Ray and Charles Ramond have found it a useful system of classification. They identify three major levels or components in the process.

1. The cognative effect.
2. The affective effect
3. The conative effect.

The cognative level involves:

Attention, awareness, comprehension and learning.

The affective component involves:

Interest, evaluation, attitude, feelings, conviction and yielding.

Lastly, the conative effect includes:

Intention, behavior and action.

The Starch, AIDA, DAGMAR (Colley 1961) learning models posit a logical sequence of cognative, affective and conative effects, namely, the sequence of attention, awareness, comprehension, learning, interest, evaluation, attitude, feeling, conviction, yielding, intention, behavior and action. Krugman's (1965) model of low involvement specifies a different sequence, namely cognative, conative, followed by the affective effect. Or the viewer is aware, comprehends, behaves or buys and then develops attitudes.

At a previous Attitude Research Conference, "Attitude Research on the Rocks," Lipstein (1968) suggested that attitude change after purchase was a form of anxiety resolution, the need to justify the purchase after the fact.

A classification scheme has merit, primarily as a function of one's objectives in the analysis. Since my interest is in measurement systems and their relationship to theories of advertising, I have found it useful to look at these issues as a function of consumer exposure to advertising. For my purposes, I have found the levels of exposure, a useful criterion since it can be conveniently related to specific measurements, systems of measurement, the theories of advertising and the content of the theories. In this approach, the controlling variable of classification is the number of exposures to the advertising.

Consider the simplest situation, the single exposure to an advertisement. In the single exposure, we have a variety of measures. There is attention, awareness of the brand, recall of the advertisement, the communications content of the ad or comprehension and some minimal level of attitude change, though the meaningful measurement of this effect due to a single exposure is subject to question. The standard measurement systems for these measures are the widely used mall testing techniques where respondents are exposed to a single commercial in a booth or van, the day after recall system of measurement concerned with attention value, recall and communications and the forced exposure approach in a theater environment.

Most of the theories of advertising start with a single exposure of the advertisement. Daniel Starch saw the communications process begin with noting or seeing the ad. The AIDA model starts with attention to the ad. DAGMAR begins with awareness. Krugman's model of how viewers attend to advertising begins with the first exposure, "What is it?" All investigators and practitioners concerned with the development and evaluation of advertising have logically started with exposure to the first advertisement. Effectively the process of selling must start here. Most of the measurement systems consider this initial exposure. The day after recall system of testing directs its primary measure to awareness and recall of the advertising. The mall system of testing is primarily concerned with communication. In any event, for the various measurement systems that are currently in use today, we find the issues of awareness, attention and recall addressed.

In the next stage of most models consideration is given to the issues of interest, communication and learning. Starch refers to reading of a print advertisement. AIDA uses the concept of interest. DAGMAR references comprehension. Krugman classifies it as "What of it?" or "Do I have an interest in the message?" There are a variety of measurements in the currently available systems which are concerned with these issues. The mall system of screening and evaluating commercials is one of the most widely used procedures for commercial evaluation. In this testing procedure, the main focus is on communication. To what degree can the viewer play back the important elements of the message and the main idea of the commercial. The issues of likes and dislikes play to the issues of interest, relevance and meaningfulness to the consumer. Some of the forced exposure systems in the theater environment provide for a second exposure and attempt to extend their measurements to some estimates of attitude change. These measures vary with the system and range from pre/post brand preference, brand lottery and a variety of attitude change measures.

Most of the models then address themselves to the effects of multiple exposure to the advertising, as well as overall

90

campaign effects. These models, namely those suggested by Starch, Colley, McGuire, Krugman, Lavidge and Steiner, and Plummer (1971) to name a few provide for all of the effects described above in the single and double exposure situations and then add other broader elements of brand image, buying behavior and attitude reinforcement following purchase. Again the research community has attempted to address these issues through various measurement systems. The custom designed tracking studies, as well as the syndicated tracking services, direct their attention to brand attributes, brand image, brand purchase and switching behavior.

On the surface, it would appear that these great variety of models of advertising and measurement systems cover all the relevant measures of viewer response and behavior to advertising. However, under more careful scrutiny, I find that there are some important variables in the advertising process that are not identified in any of these models or theories of advertising. In some sense, awareness, recall and communication are only surface measures of viewer response to advertising. There are two areas of significance which seem to have been overlooked in the modeling process: one is what I identify as dimensional reaction to commercials and the other is the negative communications; namely, misperception, miscomprehension or negative information as a function of the message.

In the next section, dimensional response of viewers to commercials and to advertising in general is discussed.

DIMENSIONS OF ADVERTISING

Mall testing is a widely used research procedure for screening and evaluating rough, as well as finished, commercials. One or more shopping malls are selected for the execution of the test. The facilities may be a mobile van, a vacant retail store or a booth. An interviewer stops shoppers in the mall and asks a number of screening questions to determine if the individual is within the target audience and eligible for interviewing. If the individual qualifies and is willing to see the commercial, he or she is lead to the screening facility and is immediately exposed to the commercial. Some researchers prefer to disguise the test by imbeding the commercial in entertainment material, in which case some preliminary questions are asked about the entertainment. The next step is to ask the viewer a number of open ended questions on the communications content of the commercial, the main idea and likes and dislikes. At this point the content of the questioning varies as a function of the preference of the research group or the issues involved in the commercial.

The findings that are discussed in this section are based

91

upon mall tests of commercials. Following the standard communications questions, a set of adjectives, i.e., interesting, was
followed by a series of agree/disagree statements about the
commercial. After the first 100 commercials had been tested by
this method, a factor analysis of the adjective check list and
the agree/disagree statments was executed. Four meaningful
factors emerged from this analysis. After the second 100
commercials were tested, a factor analysis was repeated to
determine if the same four factors emerged. In fact, the same
four factors did come out of the analysis with approximately
the same weights. These factors were named:

1. Cognative/value judgment or credibility
2. Stimulation/entertainment
3. Motivation/personal relevance
4. Empathy/self involvement or informative

The reoccurrence of these factors in repeated analysis of
different sets of commercial tests, gives some assurance of the
consistency and relevance of these factors in commercial testing. Of equal interest is that these factors appear to emerge
from other studies of advertising. Rena Bartos and Theodore
Dunn reported on the study findings of Advertising and Consumers
conducted for and published by the American Association of
Advertising Agencies. The data for that study were generated
on an entirely different basis. Yet in the analysis of those
data, similar dimensions emerge (Bartos and Dunn 1976, p. 48). One
factor is called consumer benefits or information, which is
essentially related to learning or acquiring information about
the products. A second factor in the study is credibility.
The third is entertainment value, and a fourth is tagged as
manipulation or motivation.

The AAAA study was not a copy or advertising test. It was
a national survey aimed at measuring consumer attitudes toward
advertising. It is both remarkable and important that these
same factors emerge from a totally different approach. That
these factors are present in a single ad exposure as well as
more generally in a global campaign sense clearly indicates
that they are important dimensions of the advertising process.
In a sense the models we have discussed are linear and unidi-
mensional. Behind attention, awareness and recall are a variety of consumer reactions which condition and either diminish or
magnify these measures. Whatever your theory preferences and
measurement, these dimensions will add depth.

As one of the criteria for a good theory, these measures
provide insight into a variety of commonly used measures of
advertising. Their particular values as a function of the
tested commercial can provide a basis for copy or commercial
modification.

MISCOMPREHENSION

Early in the development of an advertising campaign, those responsible for the advertising give considerable attention to the communication's content of the advertising. Almost the first question asked is "does the advertising communicate the basic message necessary to achieve the objectives of the advertising. One is also concerned with the levels of misperception or incorrect message communication which the advertising conveys. Lastly, at this early state, communications research is often viewed as a disaster check. Does the advertising communicate or create impressions which could be injurious to the brand or service.

In spite of the progress made in communications theory, advertising theory seems not to have incorporated any meaningful notions which can be used operationally to measure the communications content of advertising in a quantitative way. By content analysis of the copy, it is possible to enumerate the message or communications content of the advertising. Pragmatically, in copy testing, the researcher obtains the playback of respondents to the commercial and makes a judgement as to how effectively the commercial is communicating the message. Relatively little attention has been given to the misinformation which is generated. Practitioners have always been aware that a certain minimum level of misunderstanding occurs in commercial exposure. As a rule of thumb, misunderstanding of approximately 20% or less has been considered not objectionable. More recently, because of FTC pressure, the advertising community has begun to give some attention to the issue of misperception or miscomprehension.

In 1976, a number of professors at the University of Mannheim in Western Germany issued a small bulletin criticizing German television programming on the thesis that the public was being mislead on the basis of who was sponsoring various German television programs. Some programs had a format of information and human interest programming which was commercially sponsored and which they felt tended to misrepresent the source of sponsorship. To evaluate the substance of this claim, one of the major advertising agencies in Germany undertook a field study involving 1000 adults to determine their viewing patterns of television programs and their impressions on who sponsored these programs. Since the specific details of their viewing behavior and the sponsorship of the specific programs would have meaning only to a German audience, I have elected to omit the specific programming details. However, program sponsorship in Germany eminates from a number of sources, industry, government, political parties, trade unions, TV stations and fees paid by viewers. Based upon direct questioning of respondents, on the issue of who sponsored or paid for specific TV programs, there was very substantial variation. In the aggregate, viewers misperceived in very large order who were the sponsors of the specific programs. This misperception averaged 35%.

Eleven television programs were covered in the study. Seven were regular programming, including news reports and entertainment and four of the programs were advertising. The following table gives the percentage of viewers who classified the advertising programming material as advertising.

Parties for Election	46%
Advertising Commercials	90%
Professor Haber's Telemagazin	6%
Shopwindow on Thursday	43%

None of the programming material was classified by viewers as advertising. On the issue of source of financing of television material, respondents classified the advertising as being paid by industry as follows:

Advertising Commercials	87%
Shopwindow on Thursday	61%
Professor Haber's Telemagazin	8%
Parties for Election	0%

The misperception of who sponsored these particular programs ranged from 100% for Parties for Election to 13% for Advertising Commercials. The average misperception of sponsorship was approximately 35%. All the other programs were paid for by the TV stations. However, viewer beliefs that TV stations sponsored or paid for this programming ranged from 54% to 36%. Or their misperception of financing ranged from 46% to 74%.

These results provoked my curiosity as to whether similar levels of misperception in TV viewing occurred in the United States. I used student teams in my courses at the University to explore this issue. A series of field studies were done in the fall of 1978 and the fall of 1979. The student teams recruited viewers and asked that they watch a specific program like 60 Minutes. Specific informational content on the programming and commercials was identified by the students. In two instances they used a twenty four hour call procedure and in one, interviewing was done immediately following the viewing. In one study, 42% of the viewers misperceived or miscomprehended information in the content of the program compared to

94

a 30% level of misperception for commercials. In the other studies the level of misperception averaged approximately 30%. These studies should be viewed only as pilot investigation on the issue of miscomprehension. While the methodogy was sound, the sample of viewers was not representative. Because it was conducted by graduate students, the viewers in these studies tended to be somewhat younger than the rest of the population with substantially higher levels of educational achievement. However, the consistency of results provides a strong temptation to generalize on the average level of misperception or miscomprehension of television viewing material. Last year, the American Association of Advertising Agencies sponsored a major investigation of misperception of television commercials. I had the opportunity to see the preliminary report of study. I do not feel at liberty to discuss the findings of that study except to point out that the observed level of misperception was consistent with the findings that I have reported.

In one of the studies, the students inquired about the attitudes of the respondents on the issues that were discussed in the television commercials. Those people who had strong points of view on the issues discussed on the 60 Minute program tended to have a higher level of misperception of what was said than those who had a relatively low conviction on the issues. This would suggest that viewers tend to hear what they want to hear or tend to view material to reinforce their preconceived notions about the issues.

Interestingly, Harary and Batell (1972) used graph theory in considering the concept of negative information. If we think of negative information as an individual moving in an incorrect direction, their theoretical work suggests the possibility that negative information may result in an individual moving in an incorrect direction, their theoretical work suggests the possibility that negative information may result in individuals becoming permanently trapped in an incorrect loop from which they may never escape. In some sense, it is like prejudice and the difficulties in dislodging an individual from a prejudiced point of view.

The issue of misperception has many implications for marketing and advertising. Aside from the issues of government regulation, FTC and corrective action, there are the direct and practical implications in advertising strategy and copy execution. By way of example, in recent years a new commercial structure has evolved which I call "negative refutation." This structure of a commercial is directed to misperceptions of brands. Consider for example the problem of Lifebuoy. It is perceived as a medicinal smelling, harsh oldfashion soap. The commercial might open with the suggestion that the individual in the commercial try Lifebuoy. The expected reaction is negative: "Not that oldfashion, medicinal smelling soap. That is not for me!" The voice over might follow it with "Well, try this soap!" The actor proceeds to shower and wash with this new soap. The reaction is very positive. He asks, "What is the name of this soap?" The voice over tells him that it is new Lifebuoy. The negative information presumably has been corrected. The function of this structural device is to recruit that audience of people who have a negative and incorrect notion of Lifebuoy. The initial response is intend to generate agreement or recruitment of this audience. The trial of the new soap is intended to correct this incorrect impression. This particular type of structure is particularly suited to old brands which have a negative history which must be corrected before the newly developed product can advance in the market place. This is but one example of how we might contend with negative information.

Very briefly I am suggesting some extensions to our copy measurement systems which can add important dimensions to the development of more effective communications.

REFERENCES

Bartos, Rena and Theodore F. Dunn (1976), Advertising and Consumers, New Perspectives, American Association of Advertising Agencies.

Colley, Russell H. (1961), Defining Advertising Goals for Measuring Advertising Results, N.Y., Association of National Advertisers.

Dalbey, Homer H., Irwin Gross and Yoram Wind (1968), in Advertising Measurement and Decision Making, Patrick J. Robinson, ed., Boston: Marketing Science Institute, Allyn & Bacon.

Haskins, Jack B. (1964), "Factual Recall as a Measure of Advertising Effectiveness," Journal of Advertising Research, 4.

Joyce, Timothy (1967), What Do We Know About How-Advertising Work?, London: J. Walter Thompson Co., Ltd., Booklet 25.

Krugman, Herbert E. (1965), "The Impact of Television Advertising: Learning Without Involvement," Public Opinion Quarterly, 29, 349-356.

Krugman, Herbert E. (1972), "Why Three Exposures May Be Enough," Journal of Advertising Research, 12, 11-15.

Krugman, Herbert E., and L. E. Hartley (1970), "Passive Learning from Television," Public Opinion Quarterly, 34, 184-190.

Lavidge, Robert J., & Gary A. Steiner (1961), "A Model for Predictive Measurements of Advertising Effectiveness," Journal of Marketing, 24 (October), 59-62.

Lipstein, Benjamin (1968), "Anxiety, Risk and Uncertainty in Advertising Effectiveness Measurements," in Attitude Research on the Rocks, American Marketing Association.

McGuire, William J. (1971), "The Guiding Theories Behind Attitude Change Research," in Attitude Reaches New Highs, American Marketing Association.

Plummer, Joseph T. (1971), "A Theoretical View of Advertising Communication," The Journal of Communications, 21 (December), 315-325.

Ramond, Charles (1976), Advertising Research: The State of the Art, Association of National Advertisers, Inc.

Starch, Daniel (1923), "Testing the Effectiveness of Advertisements," Harvard Business Review.

Wells, William D., Clark Leavitt and Maureen McConnell (1971), "A Reaction Profile for TV Commercials," Journal of Advertising Research, 11 (December), 11-17.

Wilkie, William L., and Paul W. Farris (1976), Consumer Information Processing: Perspectives and Implications for Advertising, Marketing Science Institute, August.

MEDIA IMAGERY: PERCEPTION
AFTER EXPOSURE

Herbert E. Krugman, General Eelectric Company, Fairfield.

ABSTRACT

The ability of viewers to maintain attention to television for long periods of time is related to the non-tiring
qualities of right brain vigilence. Data are provided in
support of this explanation. Some implications are discussed,
especially the role of after-images, both eidetic and iconic,
in advertising.

INTRODUCTION

In a January 29, 1979 issue of Broadcasting magazine I
raised the following question about television viewing:
"Students of media behavior may yet confront the embarrassing
fact that television audiences give close attention for long
periods of time to stimuli that create no thought and little
recall. Why do they do it? What's happening?" (p. 14)

I propose to answer the question with the aid of a
hypothesis first advanced in the August 1977 issue of the
Journal of Advertising Research in which I suggested:

> "It is tempting to conclude that it is the
> right brain's picture-taking ability that
> permits the rapid screening of the environment
> -- to select what it is that the left brain
> should focus attention on." (1977, p. 11)

In this view the right brain maintains a vigil, keeps
watch on, or surveillance of the environment, and nudges the
left brain into alertness when and as needed.

Since then, in reviewing the literature on vigilance, I
found confirmation in the form of studies by the Drs. Stuart
Dimond and Graham Beaumont of the Department of Psychology at
University College in Cardiff, England which showed that left
brain attention, though much more accurate than right brain
attention in various tests of error detection, quickly tires
-- while right brain attention, though somewhat less accurate,

shows almost no fatigue (Dimond and Beaumont 1973). Thus, the so-called concentrated, selective, and conscious attention of the left brain is and should be used sparingly, as a rare and valuable resource. Meanwhile, right brain attention or vigilance, since it involves little fatigue, should no longer surprise us with its continuous activity and remarkable tolerance for sustained attention. We should accept the ability of children or adults to watch TV for zillions of hours per week, and find nothing remarkable about that physiologically. It is no more remarkable than the ability of a truck driver to drive his vehicle for many hours and to keep adequate watch on the road ahead.

Of course, both children and truck drivers, after a time, may have to fight to stay awake because of the hypnotic monotony of the situation. This is not because their brains are working hard, but because they are working very little.

Confirmation of the unique ability of the right brain to maintain sustained attention with relatively little fatigue is also provided in the form of a study conducted by Appel, Weinstein and Weinstein and reported in the August 1979 Journal of Advertising Research (Appel, Weinstein, and Weinstein 1979).

In this study thirty women were tested in groups of five and exposed to twenty pairs of television commercials three times for a total of sixty exposures. The findings reported in the journal focused on differences between reportedly high and low recall commercials but did not comment on brain hemisphere differences in response over time, i.e., over the sixty exposures.

In a subsequent discussion with the Drs. Sidney and Curt Weinstein, I asked what the left and right brain decrement had been over time. They then looked up the group means for the total thirty women tested for response to the first viewing of the twenty commercials, the second viewing, and the third viewing. Using their measure of "left-dominance index" (described on p. 12 of their published report) they were startled and surprised to tell me that the means were 18, 10 and 5 respectively. That is, left-dominance declined exponentially over time.

In the published report Table 12 on page 13 does report mean left-dominance scores for first, second and third trials for high and low recall commercials. The discussion focuses on the lack of significant differences between the commercials and ignores the left-dominance means for the low recall commercials as a group -- which decline from 10.8 to

4.2 to 3.3 for the three trials, and ignores the left-dominance means for the high recall commercials as a group which decline from 7.4 to 5.5 to 2.1.

Put another way, despite all of the micro-statistical analysis of the study a gross total record of brain activity over time showed that the left hemisphere tires and gives way to the right. In some other laboratory testing situations this would be called "adjusting to the situation," "the overcoming of the novelty effect," or simply "habituation." It has always been suspected as a problem in single exposure pretests of commercials in theater situations (e.g., Schwerin, ASI) where the initial response to the environment is atypical of natural viewing. What the group means of 18, 10 and 5 for first, second and third exposure signify here is that if you show the respondents enough commercials even in a semi-group situation, they will eventually tire to the point of achieving "natural" viewing -- with the left hemisphere relatively "turned off" and the right hemisphere remaining alert.

Although at the micro-level of analysis the authors had prematurely concluded, and I quote "...the study produced no evidence to support the belief that TV viewing is a right — hemisphere activity (p. 12)," nevertheless at the unreported macro-level of analysis the study represents the most compelling evidence to date that natural TV viewing is indeed a relatively right brain response.

Now, armed with the view that it is a right brain characteristic that sustains long periods of viewing TV, let us look at some of its implications.

At the 1979 AAPOR meeting at Buck Hill Falls, John Robinson of Cleveland State University presented some correlational data from studies of how people spend their time. He focused on time spent watching TV, and a long string of negative correlations between time with TV vs. time spent working, time spent shopping, time doing housework, etc. The one positive correlation (though low) was between time spent watching TV and time spent sleeping, especially among men. Similarly, though at a lower level, the array of coefficients for newspaper reading also showed only one positive correlation, and it too with sleeping, but only among men.

There are many questions and/or interpretations that could be put upon these data, but for me -- I have this image of the typical American male sitting in front of his TV set with a newspaper unfolded across his lap, and he -- sound asleep. The point I want to make is that each of the two media could contribute to sleep, but in a different way, the newspaper because it was fatiguing, and the television because it was relaxing.

The newspaper is described as potentially fatiguing because its physical format involves gross eye movements and highly selective choices of attention focus, i.e., left brain attention. However, as one turns the pages, skips around from topic to topic, or seeks the "continued story" in later pages, attention is rested and refreshed. That is, natural interruptions to newspaper or magazine reading are more refreshing than frustrating.

The case with TV or movies is quite different. An interruption of a movie film is highly frustrating, and a major public complaint about TV is clutter and/or commercial interruptions. The frustration involved appears to be that the left brain has been "turned on" again thereby interrupting right brain relaxation. It's as if someone turned the lights on in the middle of a film in a movie theater.

In either case, without refreshing interruption of newspaper reading or annoying interruption of TV watching, the audience may eventually fall asleep -- with the sleep of fatigue, or the sleep of relaxation.

Another set of implications of the view that the right brain sustains long periods of TV viewing is that we should take a closer look at the perception of images, both in TV and print, with special emphasis on those types of sustained perception called "after-images." But we might also describe these types of phenomena under the heading of sustained exposure.

In my 1977 talk to the ANA Media Workshop in New York, I tried to reposition the concept of perception in light of the then new brain research and suggested that advertising research try to cope with the "full range of effects," and especially to "describe the full range of exposure." The main unresolved tasks for advertising research in this area were described as three fold:

(1)   "to explore more fully the unknown territory between what we now call perception and nonperception. The "make-believe" hard line between these two is contrary to nature. Perception is not an all-or-none matter.

(2) to explore the unknown territory between what we now
     call attention and nonattention. The selective
     process of attention and nonattention involves more
     levels of attention than we like to admit.

(3) to get smarter about what lies between what we now
     call exposed and nonexposed. We may have to learn
     how to think more in terms of giving credit for
     partial exposure, for a half-exposure, for a quar-
     ter-exposure, and so on. These values also build
     up with repetition just as do full exposures."
     (1977, p. 11)

The emphasis in this call for a study of the full range
of exposure was on brief exposure because most advertising is
meant to communicate "as quick as a wink," and we could profit
from knowing more about brief and even "partial" exposure. At
the other extreme, however, we also need to push back the
limits of our concern by incorporating into the "full range of
exposure" the description of those neglected concepts of longer
exposure that also have been highlighted by new brain research.

Thus, it is within the context of the perception of
images, that I wish now to discuss those outer-limits of the
definition of exposure suggested by the after-image.

In 1930 E. R. Jaensch published his classic work on
eidetic imagery. The full title was Eidetic Imagery and Typological Methods of Investigation but the subtitle was Their
importance for the psychology of childhood. Indeed he made it
quite clear that eidetic imagery was fairly confined to children. He did predict, however, (1930, p. 23) that it would also be
more common among primitive than among civilized people.

Because of some criticism of methodology and not a little
skepticism nothing much happened for thirty years but in 1964
Haber and Haber carefully tested the whole enrollment of a New
Haven elementary school of 151 children and found that 8% or
12 children were clear Eidetikers (1964). Their after-images lasted
at least 40 seconds, and all 12 actively scanned their images
whereas none of the non-eidetic children did so in response to
any briefer after-images.

In Jaensch's time it was not known that the right hemisphere matured earlier in children than the left, and many
parents bemoaned (and still do) the loss of their child's early
artistic talents thinking it due to some fault in the educational environment. Perhaps it was, but not completely.

Partially perhaps. In the same year of the New Haven
study Leonard Doob used the Haber method to study eidetic imagery
among adults of the Ibo tribe in Nigeria (1964). Among rural
adults of the same tribe living in the provincial capital of
Enugu (population 15,000) there was very little eidetic imagery
reported, its absence presumably due to the process of accultu-
ration.

On the whole though eidetic imagery in our society is a
phenomenon of childhood and probably associated with periods of
relative right brain dominance.

There is, however, another after-image process in our
society, one which is not as dramatic as eidetic imagery in
children but which is common to us all, and this has been best
discussed by Ulric Neisser in his 1966 classic Cognitive Psychology (1966). The focus here is on what he calls iconic memory.

It was first discovered and studied using brief tachistoscopic exposures of stimuli. It was clearly demonstrated that
respondents can continue to "read" information in visual form
even after the tachistoscopic exposure is over, i.e., the
visual sensation can outlast the stimulus, for up to a second
if the post-exposure environment is relatively bright but up
to five seconds if it is dark. Please don't minimize the
importance of an extra second. You can make three eye fixa-
tions in a second and thereby absorb enough information to
engage left-brain associative responses. That is, even in the
brief exposure the response need not be passive.

To relate eidetic imagery and especially iconic memory to
our previous concern with the concepts of perception and the
limits of exposure, we would agree that "perception is an event
over time." And so we must begin again to integrate new under-
standings.

Neisser says we must begin by abandoning a set of assumptions. He says, "Even psychologists who ought to know better
have acted as if they believed (1) that the subjects visual
experience directly mirrors the stimulus pattern; (2) that his
visual experience begins when the pattern is first exposed and
terminates when it is turned off; (3) that his experience, itself a passive — if fractional — copy of the stimulus, is in
turn mirrored by his verbal report. All three of these assumptions are wrong." (1966, p. 16)

Well enough! What are we to make of all this as it
applies to advertising, to media, or to learning from media.

First, noting that all the available data on after-imagery apply to inanimate stimuli, I would suggest that print and outdoor advertising can perhaps be given more credit for some exposures which though relatively brief physically are at the same time relatively long psychologically, and active in response. I don't think those media would object.

At the same time to achieve equivalent qualities in television advertising the viewer would have to STOP and dwell on what he or she has just seen. A compromise might be a slow motion technique such as used in the famous Nice 'N' Easy Clairol commercial of 1970. Its high recall but low pupil dilation scores intrigued me at the time, and still does. However, rather than slow motion a prepared full STOP might be optimal for the advertiser, but also anxious for media executives concerned about the set being turned off or the channel switched.

Even more so, for educational television the potential for greater effectiveness lies is knowing when to slow down the action, when to program carefully prepared stopping places.

This last is of course a researchable area, perhaps a new one. We might even consider the after-imagery of children to TV when programs are interrupted, either by accident or by design.

In the beginning of this paper I suggested that the right brain maintains a vigil, keeps watch on, or surveillance of the environment, and nudges the left brain into alertness when and as needed.

For educational television I would now conclude with the suggestion that they find out how and when to nudge, and this means, to some extent, "stopping the action."

In retrospect we were probably given a good hint of this at the 1977 APA Convention when Dr. Jerome Singer of Yale reported that while pre-schoolers were more attentive to the rapid-paced structure of Sesame Street the children learned more from the slow-paced Mister Rogers (Singer et al. 1977).

REFERENCES

Appel V. S. Weinstein, and C. Weinstein (1979), "Brain Activity and Recall of TV Advertising," Journal of Advertising Research, 19 (August), 7-15.

Dimond, S. J. and J. G. Beaumont (1973), "Differences in the Vigilence Performance of the Right and Left Hemispheres," Cortex, 9, 259-265.

Doob, L. W. (1964), "Eidetic Images Among the Ibo," Ethonology, 3, 357-363.

Haber, R. N. and Haber, R. B. (1964), "Eidetic Imagery: I. Frequency," Percept. mot. Skills, 19, 131-138.

Jaensch, E. R. (1930), Eidetic Imagery and Typological Methods of Investigation, New York: Harcourt, Brace and Company.

Krugman, H. E. (1977), "Memory without Recall, Exposure without Perception," Journal of Advertising Research, (August 17), 7-12.

Neisser, U. (1966), Cognitive Psychology, New York: Appleton-Century-Crofts.

Singer, J. L. et al. (1977), "Preschooler's Comprehension and Play Behavior Following Viewing of 'Mr. Rogers' and 'Sesame Street'," Paper presented at the American Psychological Association, San Francisco (August).

DO TRENDS IN ATTITUDES PREDICT TRENDS IN BEHAVIOR?

William D. Wells, Needham, Harper & Steers Advertising, Chicago

I'd like to start with a few quotations from recent
speeches and articles that have appeared in the press.

"People are becoming increasingly concerned about their
physical appearance and health. Examples abound: jogging
is a national sport, beauty shop receipts have increased
remarkably, men are dying their hair and going to hair
stylists, the astounding growth of health spas and other
exercising facilities, health foods, etc. This is basically
an extension of the 'Age of Me' syndrome."

"Flash, fads, frills and planned obsolescence are on the
way out. Consumers are going instead for long-lasting
quality-made goods. They are moving back to time-tested
standards of design and taste, even if they have to scrimp
on some purchases in order to splurge on others."

"It's an age where people are willing to spend money on
fun, on pleasure, on me... We have had a lot of booms in
America: baby booms, inflation booms, divorce booms. Now
we're entering a personality boom--and products with a
positive personality are doing the booming."

"Certain product usage will be a sign of misanthropy and
antisocial feelings (feelings not acceptable in the We Decade).
The use of aerosol products will so qualify, as will owner-
ship of gas-guzzling cars. Tobacco will come under increased
pressure; the 'Marlboro Man' will find himself an outcast.
The use of drugs will decline radically."

"The '80s will see an increased use of tobacco, caffeine,
alcohol and marijuana, all part of the heightened incidence
of hedonism that surveys indicate is developing."

"One reason the services sector of the economy has grown
so rapidly is that many services allow consumers to purchase
time. In the decade ahead, a variety of innovative service
offerings designed to save time will flourish. Among these
offerings will be personal 'errand' services ranging from
shopping for parties to picking up consumers' dry cleaning;
wardrobe management services that have "consultants" shop
for clients according to predetermined criteria. Appointment-
based automobile repair and maintenance using "express lanes"
for certain types of routine repairs (as well as car pickup
and delivery at an extra charge); and time-management programs
for housewives and for employed women."

"Trips will be more carefully planned, and the car will be appreciated more. This may result in a slew of new products for the car and that trip. There will be more car wax, more ways of shining and washing the car, more interior and exterior decorations. The car will become an adored mistress, instead of a neglected wife."

All of these quotations have certain elements in common. They are all from prominent observers of the American scene. They all start with an observation about an attitude trend; and they all draw very specific conclusions, based upon the trend, about the future prospects of products and services. In other words, they predict changes in behavior from changes in attitudes at the aggregate level.

The wisdom of that enterprise is my topic for today.

I want to be clear about what my topic is _not_. I am not talking about cross-sectional data, in which individuals' intentions or purchases are "predicted" from their attitudes. We have all seen more or less successful predictions of this type for many years. I am _not_ talking about predicting attitudes from attitudes, or behaviors from behaviors. And I am not for the moment challenging the validity of the attitude trends set forth in any of the above quotations, even though some of them seem to me to be a little bit unbelievable.

I _am_ talking about the question of whether trends in attitudes predict trends in behavior at the aggregate level. For instance, as gasoline prices increase, will people really start washing and waxing their cars more often? As Americans become more "We oriented" (assuming that is actually happening) can we infer with any confidence that they will use fewer aerosol prodcuts, or stop smoking?

I will be using the term "predict" rather loosely, to include those cases in which attitudes and behaviors move along the same line, even though we can not be sure that the attitude caused the behavior. That is a very generous use of the word "predict," but it is a time-honored use in our inexact discipline.

And I will be using the term "attitude" very broadly to include attitudes, opinions, beliefs, and intentions. I will use the term this broadly partly because I happen to have some interesting data on beliefs and intentions, and partly because if "attitudes" so defined do not predict "behavior" in this sense, it is very difficult to see how we can have much confidence in any kind of leap from an attitude trend to a behavior trend.

107

The data I will be showing you come from a series of
"Life Style" studies we have done each year since 1975. In
these studies we have asked about two hundred questions concerning consumers' attitudes, opinions, and intentions; and
we have asked about four hundred questions concerning behavior,
including purchases of various products and participation in
various activities.

The survey was not designed to test the relationship
between attitude and behavior, so many of the attitude questions have no directly corresponding behavior questions, and
many of the behavior questions have no directly corresponding
attitudes. Also, in some instances corresponding questions
were not asked every year. Nevertheless, the data are rich
enough to allow us to look for relationships between attitude
trends and behavior trends, and to at least make some specu-
lations about why the two don't go together when they diverge.

As you might expect the answer to a simple question like
"Do trends in attitudes predict trends in behavior?" turns
out to be extraordinarily complex. But let's start with the
good news.

This graph shows the trend in positive responses to the
statement "I like to pay cash for everything I buy," for both
males and females in our sample. In all the graphs I will
be showing you, males are represented by points, and females
are represented by squares.

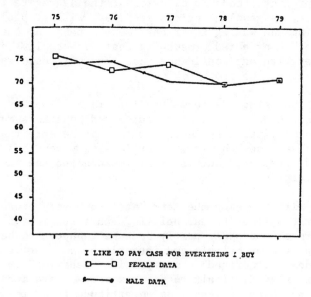

I LIKE TO PAY CASH FOR EVERYTHING I BUY
□——□ FEMALE DATA
●——● MALE DATA

As you can see, affection for cash decreases fairly consistently from 1975 to 1979. Given this trend one might well expect an increase in the use of bank charge cards, and that is just what has occurred.

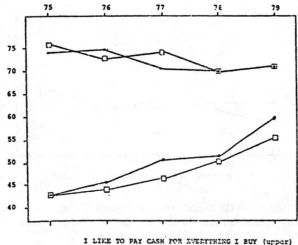

I LIKE TO PAY CASH FOR EVERYTHING I BUY (upper)

USE OF BANK CHARGE CARD (lower)

I certainly don't want to maintain that a change in attitude toward using credit was the only thing that produced the change in behavior; but if the attitude change did at least influence the behavior change the correspondence between the two trends is exactly what we would expect. And if one had observed only the trends in attitude toward using cash, one would have inferred (correctly, in this case) that use of bank charge cards would continue to go up.

So far so good. Let's take a look at another case. Here's the trend in agreement with "most big companies are just out for themselves." Here we see a general upward trend in negative attitudes toward big companies, a trend which agrees with results of many other surveys on this topic.

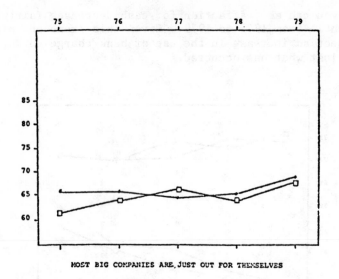

MOST BIG COMPANIES ARE, JUST OUT FOR THEMSELVES

One response that might be expected from increasing distrust of big companies would be decreasing trust in brand names. That is exactly what has happened.

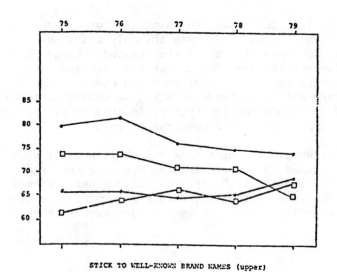

STICK TO WELL-KNOWN BRAND NAMES (upper)
MOST BIG COMPANIES OUT FOR THEMSELVES (lower)

Further, one might also expect an increasing belligerence on the part of the consumer that would lead to an increase in returning unsatisfactory products. That trend also is evident in our data.

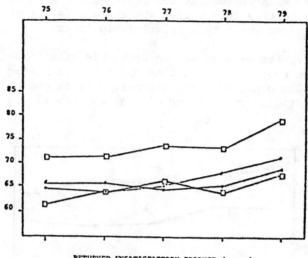

RETURNED UNSATISFACTORY PRODUCT (upper)
BIG COMPANIES OUT FOR THEMSELVES (lower)

Again, so far so good.

In line with the general lowering of trust in business we also see a declining trend in agreement with "Information from advertising helps me make better buying decisions."

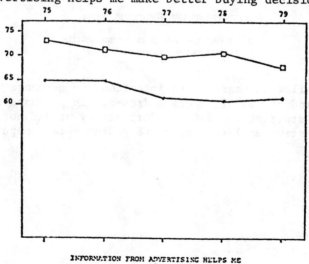

INFORMATION FROM ADVERTISING HELPS ME
MAKE BETTER BUYING DECISIONS

111

One reasonable inference from this trend would be that if people trust advertising less they trust alternative sources of information more, since information for making buying decisions must come from somewhere. This inference is supported when we look at the reported use of toll free numbers for getting information about products. I will have more to say about this relationship later.

Finally, let me show you an agreeable relationship between some expressed intentions and some purchasing behavior. Remember, for our purposes, expressions of buying intentions are included within the general concept of attitude.

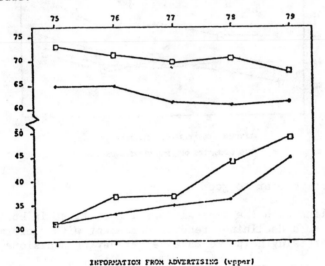

INFORMATION FROM ADVERTISING (upper)

USED A TOLL-FREE NUMBER TO GET INFORMATION
ABOUT A PRODUCT OR SERVICE (lower)

The following chart shows intentions to purchase a citizens band radio. It shows a drop-off in purchase intentions starting in 1976. Unfortunately we did not ask the question earlier, before CB radios became popular.

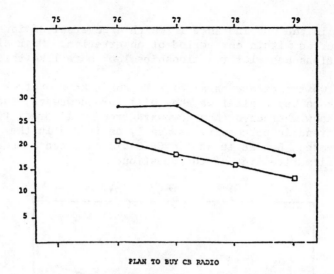

PLAN TO BUY CB RADIO

When we look at CB purchases, we see that purchases actually increased rather sharply between '76 and '77, as would be expected from the fact that substantial numbers of respondents had been expressing positive intentions a year earlier. But starting with '77 the drop in intentions apparently "caught up" with the market and purchasing deteriorated.

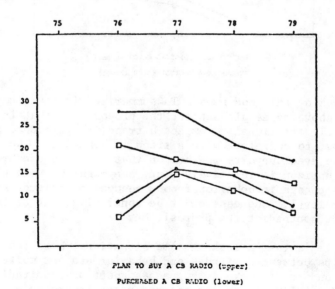

PLAN TO BUY A CB RADIO (upper)
PURCHASED A CB RADIO (lower)

113

This is the one instance in which a reversal of intentions occurred within our period of observation. Most of
the intentions-behavior relationships look more like this:

The two trends are parallel. We don't know whether
intentions to buy digital watches will turn downward, and
we don't know whether such a downward trend will predict a
downward trend in purchasing as neatly as it did in the
CB radio case. But at least the CB radio case can be counted
on the affirmative side of the question.

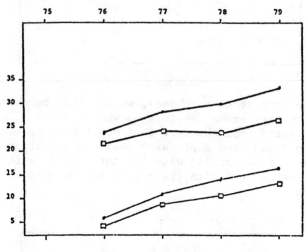

PLAN TO BUY A DIGITAL WATCH (upper)
PURCHASED A DIGITAL WATCH (lower)

Enough of the good news. To summarize, it seems to me
that the above cases all support the proposition that it is
not entirely irrational to expect a trend in attitudes, or
intentions, to correlate with a trend in behavior. The CB
radio case even supports the notion that when the consumer's
planning horizon is relatively long, one might be able to
predict a change in behavior from a change in attitude at the
aggregate level. One case can't be conclusive, but at least
it doesn't contradict the proposition.

Now let's take a look at some situations where the relationships between attitudes and behavior are not quite so
elegant, and try to make some guesses about why contradictions
occur. Hopefully we can get to some general hypotheses about
when attitudes and behavior are likely to agree and when they
are likely to disagree.

This chart shows no change in agreement by women with the statement "I like to feel attractive to members of the opposite sex."

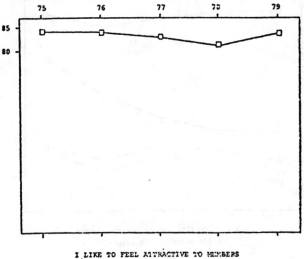

I LIKE TO FEEL ATTRACTIVE TO MEMBERS
OF THE OPPOSITE SEX

Unfortunately for our desire for a nice relationship between attitudes and behavior, this trend was accompanied by a slight _increase_ in use of lipstick and nailpolish,

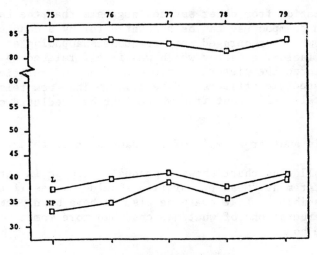

I LIKE TO FEEL ATTRACTIVE TO MEMBERS
OF THE OPPOSITE SEX (upper)

USE LIPSTICK MORE THAN ONCE A DAY   (L)

USE NAIL POLISH ONCE A WEEK OR MORE   (NP)

115

and a very <u>sharp</u> increase in use of shampoo.

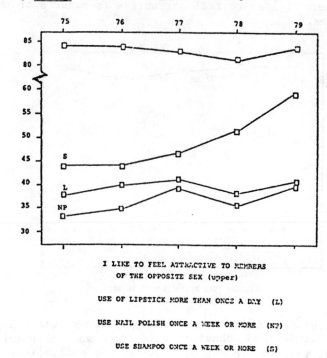

I LIKE TO FEEL ATTRACTIVE TO MEMBERS
OF THE OPPOSITE SEX (upper)

USE OF LIPSTICK MORE THAN ONCE A DAY   (L)

USE NAIL POLISH ONCE A WEEK OR MORE   (NP)

USE SHAMPOO ONCE A WEEK OR MORE   (S)

Information from other sources suggests that the rapid
increase in shampoo use can be accounted for by a change in
hairstyles which encouraged more frequent shampooing at home.
Thus a new factor, a factor which was itself related to hairstyles, entered the picture to produce a lack of relationship
between a specific attitude and behavior. This new relationship is totally different from what might be predicted on the
basis of a naive one-to-one inference.

Here is another example of the same sort of thing.

The following chart shows a gradual <u>increase</u> in agreement
with the statement "Meal preparation should take as little
time as possible." Like everyone else we have been picking
up the reverberations of what happens when more women work
outside the home.

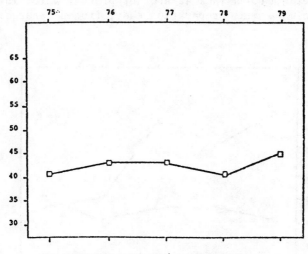

MEAL PREPARATION SHOULD TAKE AS LITTLE TIME AS POSSIBLE

From this upward trend it would be perfectly reasonable to expect increased use of frozen pizza, a product which is intended to make meal preparation easy. The relationship is there, and it looks pretty good.

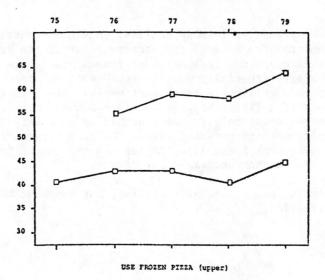

USE FROZEN PIZZA (upper)

MEAL PREPARATION SHOULD TAKE AS LITTLE
TIME AS POSSIBLE (lower)

But let's take a look at another product which is also intended to make meal preparation easy, frozen vegetables.

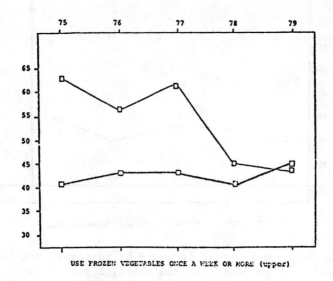

USE FROZEN VEGETABLES ONCE A WEEK OR MORE (upper)

MEAL PREPARATION SHOULD TAKE AS LITTLE
TIME AS POSSIBLE (lower)

Here we see a precipitous decline. Again an extraneous factor seems to have entered the picture. During the years shown on this chart the real price of frozen vegetables increased sharply, especially when compared with the cost of other ways to simplify preparation of meals. Also, to get ahead of myself a little bit, we should remember that frozen vegetables represent only one of a number of acceptable ways of shortening meal preparation time. The link between the desire to make meal preparation easier and the use of frozen vegetables is neither necessary nor direct.

Now let's take a look at a similar, but somewhat more complex situation.

This line shows a steady increase from 1976 to 1979 in agreement with the statement, "Aerosol sprays are harmful to us and our environment."

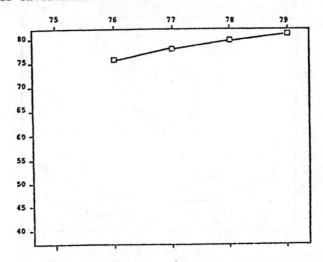

AEROSOL SPRAY CANS ARE HARMFUL TO US AND OUR ENVIRONMENT

This trend suggests that consumers were translating this concern directly into behavior, at least until 1978.

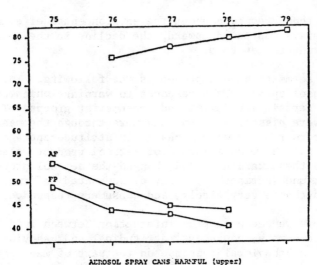

AEROSOL SPRAY CANS HARMFUL (upper)

USE AIR FRESHENER SPRAYS ONCE A WEEK OR MORE (AF)

USE FURNITURE POLISH IN SPRAY CAN ONCE A WEEK OR MORE (FP)

But look what happened in 1979.

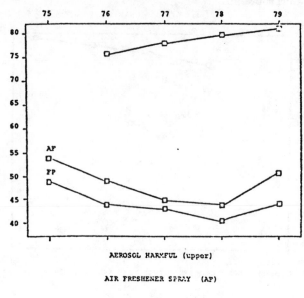

AEROSOL HARMFUL (upper)

AIR FRESHENER SPRAY (AF)

FURNITURE POLISH SPRAY (FP)

Even though concern about the environmental effects of aerosol sprays continued upward, the decline in these two aerosol products reversed.

What seems to have happened is the following. The concern about aerosol sprays was a response to warnings which originated with certain government and consumerist groups. These warnings were disseminated to consumers through the mass media, and consumers reacted with a change in attitude and a change in behavior. The manufacturers of aerosol products also responded to these warnings, and changed the aerosol propellent to make it unobjectionable. They disseminated information about this change very widely, and consumers responded.

So here we see a complex interaction between information given to consumers, consumers' attitudinal and behavioral responses, a behavioral response on the part of manufacturers, and a second behavioral response on the part of consumers. The first behavioral response from consumers was "predictable" from the attitude data; the second was not.

120

Another way to find a disagreement between an attitude and a behavior is to make a literal interpretation of an attitude measurement which is itself embedded in a larger and more pervasive situation. Here is a trend in agreement with the statement, "Everyone should use mouthwash to help prevent bad breath." As you can see the trend is definitely downward.

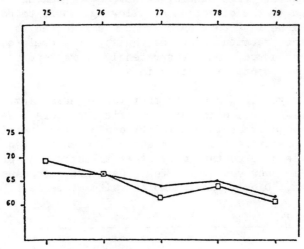

EVERYONE SHOULD USE A MOUTHWASH TO
HELP CONTROL BAD BREATH

Here is mouthwash <u>use</u> as reported in '77, '78 and '79 by females, '78 and '79 by males. Unfortunately, we do not have corresponding data from earlier years. It is obvious that at least from '78 to '79 the attitude trend and the behavior trend were moving in opposite directions.

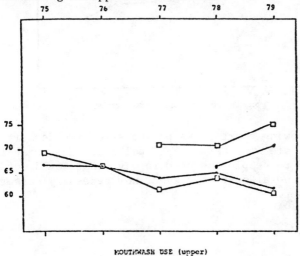

MOUTHWASH USE (upper)

EVERYONE SHOULD USE (lower)

121

What has happened here, I think, is that reactions to the statement, "Everyone should use mouthwash to help prevent bad breath" were influenced by general consumer reactions against proscriptions. Every attitude statement in our study which says flatly that people should or should not do something has trended downward. Like others, we have been picking up a general trend in the direction of allowing people to do their own thing. I believe that this trend has affected the responses to the statement about mouthwash, and permitted an attitude as measured, and the apparently corresponding behavior to move in opposite directions.

It has often been observed that very general attitudes do not correlate well with very specific behaviors. We saw an example of that in the relationship between attitudes toward meal preparation and purchase of frozen vegetables. Our Life Style data contain many other illustrations of this point. Let me show you just a few. Here are responses to the statement, "Dinner isn't complete without dessert."

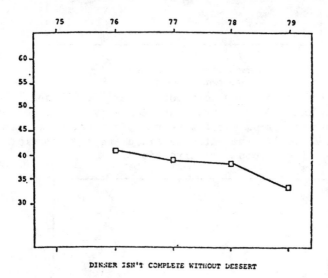

DINNER ISN'T COMPLETE WITHOUT DESSERT

The following chart shows purchases of two dessert items, both of which are increasing. The point is that these items can be served to people and used in ways that would not contradict the general sentiment about how necessary dessert is after dinner.

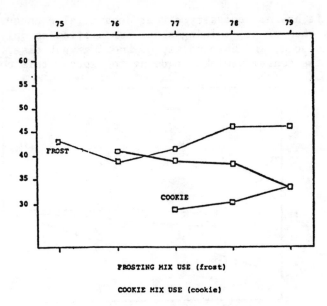

FROSTING MIX USE (frost)

COOKIE MIX USE (cookie)

DINNER ISN'T COMPLETE WITHOUT DESSERT (heavy line)

Here are consumers' concerns about sugar, expressed as agreement with the statement, "I am concerned about how much sugar I eat" -- a general upward trend. From this trend one might reasonably expect some down trend in consumption of heavily sugared items.

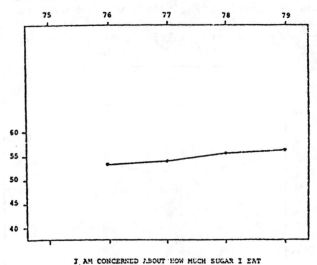

I AM CONCERNED ABOUT HOW MUCH SUGAR I EAT

But look what has happened to consumption of Lifesavers and of those sugary villains, Ding Dongs, Ho Ho's and Twinkies. Again, the point is that concern about sugar is a very abstract

123

concept. It has no necessary direct behavioral consequences, especially when we are talking about consumption of only two sugared products, and have no way of knowing what else, if anything, the consumer might be doing to express this concern.

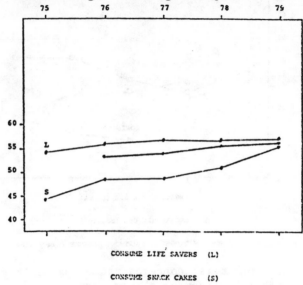

CONSUME LIFE SAVERS (L)

CONSUME SNACK CAKES (S)

I AM CONCERNED ABOUT HOW MUCH SUGAR I EAT

Here is agreement with, "No matter how fast our income goes up, we never seem to get ahead." Agreement with this statement was relatively high in 1975 when we were just coming out of our last bout with recession and inflation. It dropped as inflation moderated, and in 1979 it was higher than it has ever been.

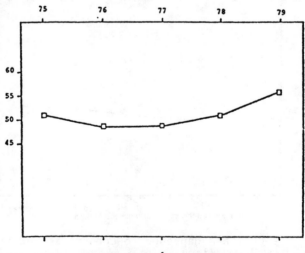

NO MATTER HOW FAST OUR INCOME GOES UP
WE NEVER SEEM TO GET AHEAD

124

What would we infer from this curve? We would infer
that people would use price-off coupons more, that they would
shop a lot for specials and that they would check prices even
on small items--or at least they would report that they were
doing so. Here are the trends.

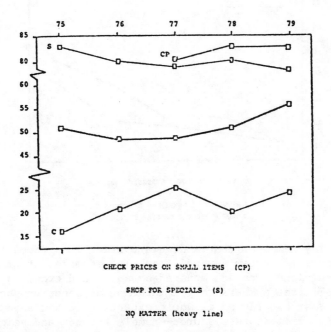

CHECK PRICES ON SMALL ITEMS (CP)

SHOP FOR SPECIALS (S)

NO MATTER (heavy line)

USE PRICE-OFF COUPONS ONCE A WEEK OR MORE (C)

Not only do the trends in behavior not agree with the
very clear and regular trend in attitude; the trends in
behavior don't even agree with each other. General attitude,
specific behavior go in divergent ways.

Finally, just to give one more example, I would like
to return to the chart on consumers' attitudes toward
advertising.

125

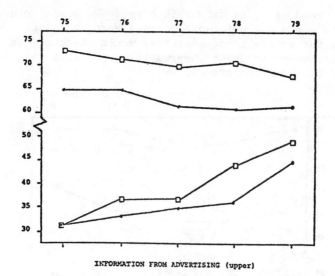

INFORMATION FROM ADVERTISING (upper)

USED A TOLL-FREE NUMBER TO GET INFORMATION
ABOUT A PRODUCT OR SERVICE (lower)

You may remember that a downward trend in agreement with "Information from advertising helps me make better buying decisions" was accompanied by an upward trend in the use of toll free numbers to get information about products and services, exactly as we would expect. Now how about information from another source--namely friends and neighbors? If people trust advertising less, they ought to be trusting their friends and neighbors more. But that is not the case.

The following chart is agreement with the statement, "I often seek out the advice of my friends regarding brands and products."

We have now seen a number of instances in which trends in behavior flowed nicely along with trends in attitudes, and a number of instances in which attitudes and behavior did not seem to agree at all. What makes the difference?

126

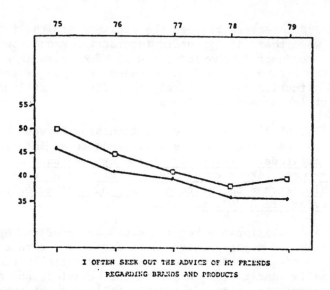

I OFTEN SEEK OUT THE ADVICE OF MY FRIENDS
REGARDING BRANDS AND PRODUCTS

Attitudes seem to predict behavior best when the attitudes are very specific, and when the attitude can be enacted in only one way. Perhaps the best example of specificity is the prediction of purchases from purchase intentions.

When we begin to get less specific--for instance when we attempt to infer use of bank charge cards from attitudes toward credit or the use of toll free numbers from mistrust of advertising--we begin to add substantial risk to the prediction. If a consumer doesn't pay cash for a product, he or she still has a number of options, only one of which is to use a bank charge card. If a consumer trusts advertising less he or she can turn to other sources of information, and the availability of multiple information sources loosens the connection between the general attitude and any one of the possible consequences. When the attitude becomes very abstract, such as a general concern about sugar consumption, everything is up for grabs. It is extremely difficult to guess what, if anything, the consumer will do about this attitude, and it is especially difficult to jump from the attitude to behavior with respect to any specific sugared product.

In short, the connection between an attitude and a behavior is most likely to be tight when the attitude is specific rather than general, when the connection is direct, and when the attitude can lead to one and only one behavior.

When is the connection likely to break down? We have seen at least four such situations. Attitudes and behavior are likely to diverge when the attitude is very general, when other factors intervene between the attitude and the inferred behavior, when there is a complex interaction among consumers' attitudes, consumers' behaviors, and manufacturers' behaviors; and when the attitude itself is embedded in a larger and more pervasive situation that is likely to affect the attitude measurement in unpredictable ways.

This way of looking at the relationships between trends in attitudes and trends in behaviors leads to an interesting paradox. <u>Attitude measurements of the type we have been discussing are most likely to be most useful when an expected relationship between an attitude trend and a behavior trend and a behavior trend does not occur.</u>

When the relationship between attitude trend and behavior trend is nice and tight—as it was in our credit card case, for example—the attitude measurement is essentially redundant. What we really want to know about is the behavior, and a perfectly correlated attitude doesn't tell us a lot more.

But when attitude trends and behavior trends diverge, especially when the attitudes and behaviors have the characteristics that would lead us to expect a tight relationship—we are led into a search for the other factors that might be producing the behavior. In this search, the availability of the attitude data allows us to eliminate one of the possible explanations for the behavior we are trying to understand.

On the other hand, attitude measurements are <u>least</u> likely to be useful when we try to infer specific behaviors from trends in broad, general attitudes. The dice are really loaded against us there. In that situation, our chances for a successful leap from attitude to behavior are very slight indeed.

All of this sounds pretty obvious, and maybe it is. But if it <u>is</u> obvious, why do intelligent people persist in inferring the growth of health spas from "The Age of Me?" Why do they try to predict a desire for quality goods from the growth of inflation? Why is willingness to spend money on fun said to be the product of a "personality boom?" Why is a decline in the use of drugs the result of a growth in the "We Decade?" And why do <u>we</u> listen attentively when someone predicts increased use of car wax from a projected increase in the cost of gasoline?

ATTITUDE RESEARCH IN THE EIGHTIES:
A MATURING DISCIPLINE FACES A DIFFICULT DECADE

Phil Levine, Reva Korad & Associates, New York

ABSTRACT

The coming information revolution gives attitude researchers the unique opportunity of becoming an important part of the decision process.

Will we take advantage of this opportunity?

How can we take advantage of this opportunity?

The future of our discipline depends mightily on the answers to these questions.

When I started writing this speech I was Executive Director of Research at Ogilvy & Mather. When I finished writing it, I was a partner in Reva Korda & Associates. And I have to tell you, I came very close to re-titling this speech "A Maturing Researcher Faces A Difficult Decade".

I'm looking forward to my new job with great enthusiasm, particularly since it's the first new agency I can remember that's been founded as a partnership of creative and research.

But enough of that. On to the subject at hand.

Living in total isolation is the only way any of us could possibly have avoided seeing or hearing at least one soothsayer's predictions about the Decade of the '80 s.

The future has been forecast demographically, attitudinally, behaviorally, etc., etc.

But if there is one phenomenon that has been universally predicted for the Decade of the '80 s, it is the technological revolution. A technological revolution that many claim is the outgrowth of our massive commitment to space exploration over the last two decades.

A recent AT&T advertisement puts some perspective on this revolution as it relates to information delivery. This advertisement, entitled "The Knowledge Business," says, in part,

"Over 30 years ago, C.E. Shannon formulated information theory, a way to predict how much information can be transmitted in electronic communications. It was a landmark in the knowledge business."

"Recently sociologists such as Daniel Bell began discussing the emergence of knowledge workers and the implications of the knowledge business for all of society. It is only now that the business applications of information management utilizing advanced communications are being fully realized, increasing efficiency, lowering costs, improving profits."

"Theoretical knowledge, codified and turned to practical applications."

"The time is right for corporations to discuss the future as it is practiced now. With lasers, satellite communications, magnetic bubble memories, fiber optics, microelectronics."

The ad concludes by saying:

"We are insight. We are change. We are the future. And we can put it to work for your business. The knowledge business."

In fact, this technology is already having an undeniable impact on attitude research -- on the way we conduct it, on the way we analyze it, on the way we report it.

Already we are using:

- record retrieval systems, with microfilm, microfiche, and magnetic tape, card or disc storage capability, that allow us to retrieve research already conducted that may help us with current projects (thus is the wheel not reinvented each time we decide to conduct research);

- word processing systems, which save money and time by editing and/or rewriting questionnaires and other research materials almost instantly;

- cathode ray tube technology, that eliminates the present paper questionnaire and allows for instantaneous tabulation;

- two-way television feedback systems, where respondents can immediately answer questions about various stimuli they see on their television sets;

- OCR (or optical character recognition) machines, to "read" numbers and hand-printed numerics -- less expensive, time consuming than using coding clerks.

And there is more, much more on the way.

I submit, it is this information revolution which places attitude research right smack at the crossroads. Crossroads that can take us much closer to the professional role we seek and deserve. The alternative would be, once again, to slide sulkingly into the background, blaming everyone but ourselves when people fail to acknowledge the significance of our contribution.

It wasn't very long ago that we in attitude research were simply the collectors of data. We gathered and reported numbers. What the numbers meant was left to other people to decide.

More recently, researchers came to function as transmitters of information. We were allowed to define trends and interpret the significance of the data we collected.

Though decision-making came to be more dependent on our interpretations and observations, we were still reluctant to assign values to the data; to become more active in decision-making itself.

And that is where we find ourselves today. As I said, at the crossroads.

So where do we go from here?

131

Clearly, we can't go backwards. The time is
almost here when any reasonably intelligent clerk
will be able to collect the information our
businesses depend on. Nobody needs an attitude
researcher to do that.

Or do we stay where we are, continuing our half-
passive, half-active role, immersing ourselves in
the information, stopping just short of making a
major contribution to the decision-making process?

I say no -- to both courses.

We've already completed two historic steps in
what I consider the maturing process of the attitude
research discipline. From data collectors to information transmitters to ... what?

To professionals who provide not just data, not
just information, but intelligence. The next historic step is for attitude researchers to become
major contributors to the decision-making process.
Time for us to become partners who analyze data and
make recommendations based on those analyses.
Partners whose training, experience and perspective
make them uniquely well qualified to participate.

All well and good. But as a discipline, are we
ready? I'm going to hedge a bit on that one because
the answer is yes and no.

So on to a bit of appraising -- or self-apprais-
ing something we in attitude research do far too
little. If the American Bar Association and the
American Dental Association can play an active role
in determining the future direction of their disciplines, so can we. In fact, it's about time we
did.

I'd like us to have a look at where we stand in
some key areas.

Let me start with our most important resource,
people.

From a people point-of-view, I think we are a
lot more ready than we have ever been to meet the
challenge of the '80 s.

132

An attitude researcher these days is less and less the cloistered intellectual doing tabulations in a cubicle. More and more, he or she is the member of a team of decision-making professionals. Professionals from a wide variety of disciplines.

We're better managers now. We're more introspective, too, giving more thought to the kinds of research we conduct, and how we conduct it -- and why.

We are looking for people who are able to relate to other researchers, to clients, and to colleagues in their company.

The kind of person we will need to meet the challenge of the 1980s will have the following profile:

- has a total commitment to objectivity and integrity, and has courage under fire;

- takes the larger view, but comes in close when necessary;

- has professional stature -- technical competence and a solid reputation in the business;

- has personal stature, too -- maturity, confidence, and a businesslike manner and appearance;

- identifies with the business he or she works in not just research;

- is a good communicator -- in person and on paper;

- has good managerial skills, with the ability to relate well to different kinds of people and the ability to apportion time efficiently.

And we have something else working for us: all of a sudden, some of the brightest graduates of our best universities are looking favorably at research as a career. Now if only some of us would train this talent -- rather than waiting to pick them off as soon as they are trained -- we might get enough real talent in place to meet the challenge that face us in the '80s.

But in order to achieve the high ground I've just talked about, we have to mend some of the basics we have let slip.

1. We will have to go back to designing questionnaires respondents can answer -- not questionnaires that fit the requirements of our analytic techniques. We'll have to pretest our questionnaires more rigorously, too -- and more often. We'll pay more attention to the types of scales we use.

   We will have to stop the unforgivable practice of allowing the junior members of our profession to be most responsible for buying research. Quite simply, this practice is leading to a proliferation of bad research.

   There seems to be some stigma attached to being the one who buys the research. Senior people shun it like the plague. But how many junior researchers have the knowledge -- or, indeed, the security -- to select and work with the real professionals of our business? Can we really afford to substitute their judgment for the judgment of more seasoned, experienced members of our profession?

   And though everybody defends this practice by saying they're supervising their underlings, how much supervision are they really doing? We've got to stop paying lip service to this problem and do something about it.

2. We will have to quash the growing tendency to misuse group session research.

   At a time when inflation is sending research costs through the roof, an understandable solution is to save money by halting the research effort after only a few group sessions.

Inflation is real. Increased costs can lead
to budgeting problems.

But the answer must not be to substitute bad
or inappropriate research for no research.
We must allow judgment to rule when we can't
afford to do what's called for.

Group sessions should be used to develop a
list of benefits that may be important; to
develop vocabulary and situations, gain fresh
insights, and help the creative process.

They shouldn't be used to evaluate the
importance of various benefits or to discover whether advertising executions
communicate what they're supposed to.

In short, group sessions should be used
appropriately -- not to save money. And,
now incidentally, there may be alternative
techniques available that can give us the
right answers without breaking our budgets.

3. We will have to be more involved in over-
   seeing the use of research in adversary
   proceedings. That's a whole new phenomenon.
   And whether we like it or not, attitude
   research will be used in legal proceedings
   much more frequently in the 1980s.   But
   we're the experts in this area. We, not the
   lawyers, must establish guidelines for the
   proper use of attitude research in the
   courts.

4. We will have to develop a self-policing
   mechanism because there's a growing Faustian
   tendency in our ranks. I speak of those
   senior researchers who are selling their
   souls in the courtrooms as expert witnesses.

   "How do I satisfy the lawyers' requirements?"
   they ask themselves -- not, "How do I satisfy
   the ethics of my profession?" Shame on them.

   All right. Enough wrist-slapping. Let's
   have a look at the methodological trends that
   will surface in this new decade.

135

I'm pleased to report that in the 1980s all
signs point to a continuance of the trend
toward the programmed approach to attitude
research in place of the project approach.
Rather than spend all available funds on one
very big and expensive study, the tendency
will be to do a number of studies, with each
study providing input to the next stage.

Consistent with this approach, more and more
clients will ask for research program proposals rather than research project proposals.

There's an interesting side-benefit to this
trend: The programmed approach makes us more
resistant to fads. We are virtually immune
to the "everybody's doing it" urge that has
plagued us so often in the past.

5. We have to get back to using experimental
   designs. Greater use of Latin Squares,
   Factorals, Randomized Blocks, Greco Latin
   Squares, and so on.

   Though these designs were used often and
   very effectively in the early and mid-1960s,
   we seem to have forgotten how helpful they
   can be until fairly recently.

   Who knows how many other so-called new
   techniques will resurface when we re-examine
   the literature on experimental design? Let
   the ideas flourish; I think we're on the
   threshold of a very innovative period in
   research.

6. Greater use of mathematical models is already gaining greater acceptance. There are
   obvious advantages in being able to "model"
   a process. Models provide a better understanding of the interrelationships between
   variables. They lead to more efficient and
   effective data collection. And they enable
   you to game your own activities and those of
   the competition.

   And while some have said the marketing process is too complex to be modeled, we've
   found models such as Hendry, Sprinter and

Assessor quite helpful. I think the next
five years will produce major breakthroughs
in this area. Breakthroughs, particularly,
in the use of attitudinal data in model
building.

Research and researchers are becoming more and
more involved in the decision-making process.
More emphasis on the use of attitudinal data
and less emphasis on the elegance of the
research design, are paying off. But we still
have a long way to go.

Yes, the attitude research discipline is at a
crossroads.

A time when senior practitioners of attitude
research cannot sit and listen passively to
techniques and methodologies being presented.

It's time we took a more active role in policing
our disciplines practices. It's time we started
guarding our discipline from the heavy hands of
the law.

It's time we gave a discipline that's been so
good to us something in return.

RETRIEVING UTILITIES FROM
INDUSTRIAL BUYERS WITHOUT
BRAIN SURGERY OR CONJOINT MEASUREMENT

William C. Cook
E. I. du Pont de Nemours & Co., Inc., Wilmington

ABSTRACT

Industrial marketing research studies are presented which take advantage of certain characteristics of industrial buyers to simplify trade-off research methodology to permit lower-cost interviews.

INTRODUCTION

Brain surgery is not an acceptable way of measuring the contribution of a specific feature to the value of the overall product offering, that is, the utility of that feature. For some studies of the buying behavior of Du Pont's industrial customers, conjoint measurement is just as infeasible as brain surgery. My talk deals with how we, at Du Pont, have obtained a quantitative assessment of the utility, or in Du Pont parlance perceived value, buyers attach to various components of a product offering in situations where conjoint measurement is not possible.[1]

I use the term conjoint measurement to refer to the scaling technique in which subjects express evaluations between pairs or rank order a number of complex stimuli like multiattribute product descriptions. It represents one of various methods in which subjects are asked to trade off one attribute against another (Green and Rao 1971). By using balanced experimental designs, usually fractional factorial designs, conjoint measurement makes it possible to develop ratio scales on the basis of simple ordinal judgments and to decompose the values of the overall product offering into its component parts.

These experimental design and scaling tasks are often quite complex. Furthermore, from the perspective of

---

[1] I want to acknowledge here my indebtedness to my interested and helpful colleagues at Du Pont whose contribution to my own thinking has been substantial. I am especially indebted to J. L. Piech for his mathematical contributions and to I. Gross for his insights on perceived value.

questionnaire construction and data collection methodology, the typical application of conjoint measurement involves much effort in the structuring of the set of attributes to be studied and in the descriptors used for the various levels of each attribute. In spite of the effort involved, the payoffs in both consumer and industrial marketing research have been large enough to motivate a significant trend toward the use of this research tool.

We at Du Pont have asked ourselves, "Do our industrial marketing problems require such a complicated methodology?" Perhaps so. We want to use a measuring device which is sophisticated enough for the number and complexity of the attributes we have. The high technology and strong service orientation of most Du Pont businesses mean assessing the perceived value of R&D and Technical Service is often as important as measuring the perceived value of a product's physical attributes. Measuring the perceived value of such intangible attributes is an even more difficult task for the researcher than is assessing the value of simple physical characteristics of the product. Yet, there are certain aspects of industrial marketing problems which permit simplifying the task to some extent.

A significant difference between the purchase-decision making behavior of the industrial buyer and the typical consumer is the consistency with which the industrial buyer exhibits higher utility for lower price. This rational economic behavior of the industrial buyer is reinforced by a greater knowledge of the product attributes than is the case with most consumers. The implication of this difference in industrial and consumer buying is that we can obtain more direct measures of the industrial buyer's perceived values, and we can often simplify the attribute presentation. The driving force for simplifying things is not just to make the researcher's job easier. A simpler research methodology pays off in terms of the ease of communicating the research results and their implications to the client, the industrial marketing manager.

The reference to brain surgery in my title has the unfortunate connotation that I consider the primary role relationship to be that of the researcher and the buyer as the surgeon and patient. In fact, I consider the real patient to be the harried marketing manager and the role of the marketing researcher to be more like that of the humble psychotherapist. It is also my intention today to give consideration to this important relationship between the marketing manager and the marketing researcher.

The origin of my reference to brain surgery is an image which frequently comes to me as I contemplate attitude research. This image depicts a researcher lifting off the top of a buyer's head and taking readings from a set of gauges neatly arrayed inside it. One gauge, set apart slightly and larger than the others, is connected to all the other gauges and provides a single integrated measure of the value of the stimulus which the buyer is contemplating.

My reflection on this image confronts me with a paradox in my thinking about attitudinal research. It seems to me that if there is information about the buyer's decision process which is accessible to me in some way, then that information must also be available to the buyer. I hypothesize from such musing that I should be able to obtain direct measures of these utilities by asking the right questions of the buyer. At the same time, I am concerned that in the process of "reading his gauges" the buyer may alter the values registered there. This notion of interference produced by introspection bothers me. It suggests to me that perhaps in the process of my looking into the buyer's decision-making activity I, too, may change what is occurring.

I attempt to resolve this paradox by assuring myself that the cognitive activities I am asking the buyer to engage in during my interview are as close as possible to those involved in his purchase decision-making task. Conjoint measurement permits marketing researchers to assess the utility of product attributes while engaging the subject in cognitive activities at least similar to those involved in the actual purchasing decisions. I think this is a significant contribution to attitude measurement.

I am not convinced that abstract attributes are always meaningful to the subject apart from the concrete descriptions of categories or sets of labels which define the assumed continua along which they are spread. Ahtola (1975) has criticized the Fishbein model on similar grounds. He has pointed out that the simple definition in a Fishbein-type model of such attributes as sweetness or carbonation render their goodness ratings difficult to interpret. Ahtola has recommended that instead of single measures of strength of belief and goodness for each attribute, we obtain multiple ratings using several levels or categories for each attribute.

A concretely illustrated dimension is more meaningful for the marketing manager as well as the buyer. The implications for what action to take are much clearer when delivery time has been translated into specific terms like "95% of deliveries within two weeks," "95% of deliveries within one week," etc., than when one is told that 85% of the subjects gave speed of delivery a "+2" rating.

Presenting more than one level of an attribute can be said to provide a frame of reference within which to evaluate attributes at a specified level. Similarly, presenting more than one attribute at a time provides a needed context within which to evaluate a given attribute. This is obvious if there is assumed to be an interaction among the attributes. I would argue that even where no interaction is assumed to exist, there is a need to represent the other attributes to create the appropriate cognitive set for the buyer to make the requested judgment. By appropriate cognitive set, I mean one that elicits the same cognitive activity which would be a part of the normal purchase decision. This is another contribution of the conjoint measurement approach in that several attributes are usually presented at the same time.

The presentation to the subject of large numbers of attributes at one time may, however, be a means by which users of conjoint measurement alter the normal cognitive functioning. There is ample evidence (Bettman 1979) that the decision rules a subject is using may be changed if the information load produced by the stimuli presented is much greater than what is typically experienced. Conjoint measurement with a very large number of attributes may be measuring very atypical decision-making behavior. Even though the list of attribute levels may be written down and placed before the subject, his information-handling capacity may still be exceeded if the list is quite long.

The response which the buyer is asked to make in the typical conjoint measurement study is a preference response. This may be a simple pair-wise preference task or a complex task involving rank ordering of 30 or more stimuli, but it is still a matter of expressing a preference for one combination of attributes over another. Either of these preference measures is a closer analogue to the actual purchase task than is an importance rating. Even though reality constraints may result in a difference between preference and actual purchase behavior, the greater likelihood that a preference measure is tapping into the same cognitive activities involved in the actual purchase decision makes it the preferred measure for this researcher.

Conjoint measurement, as I see it, has a lot to recommend its use besides its ability to provide ratio-scale measures of utility from simple preference measures. It involves

stimuli which are processed in ways which resemble actual purchase decisions. It involves a preference response which is
very similar to the response we are trying to predict.

Why then have we at Du Pont not used conjoint measurement
for all our perceived value studies of industrial product
offerings? In many of our industrial businesses, the marketing research budget is too small to provide for personal interviews with the widely dispersed customer population involved.
For many of our industrial clients, budgetary limitations are
coupled with timing pressures and/or lack of a trade show
where less expensive interviews might be obtained.

I want to describe for you three research techniques with
which we have experimented and which are adaptable to WATS
line telephone interviewing. Two of these techniques were
investigated in the same study and offer a chance to compare
the results of the scalings obtained. Although it may not be
essential we have used computer-assisted interviewing to allow
us the opportunity to randomize the selection and ordering of
stimulus pairs to be used for a given subject. We believe
that where incomplete blocking designs are used randomization
to reduce order bias is very desirable. In this case, we also
felt that the complexity of the interviewer's task might result in errors which would degrade the quality of the information obtained. Computer-assisted interviewing reduced that
risk substantially.

ATTRIBUTE TRADE-OFF

This first study is a good one for illustrative purposes
in that it is representative of so many of the business problems on which we consult at Du Pont:

- Du Pont is a major supplier to the market of
  interest;

- Du Pont's product offering was at the high
  end of the spectrum in terms of quality,
  technical expertise and price;

- Marketing management was not considering
  major product alterations but wanted to
  optimize their price/attribute trade-off;

- Marketing research had not been used in a
  carefully planned way or with any frequency
  in the past.

142

Before I get into the methodological details of the study, let me tell you a few specific things about the business. To mask the identity of the actual product involved, I will refer to a fictitious industrial chemical product, "Hypothet". Although the product is a fabrication, the essence of the product attributes and the business needs involved have been preserved.

The Du Pont specialty product Hypothet is used exclusively in one industry. There are a small number of competitors offering very similar products in that market. While the competitive products are similar, there are differences in the total offerings of the competitors. The Du Pont offering has consistently been granted a premium price by the market although the amount has tended to decline over the years.

When we were contacted, Hypothet marketing management was concerned that a recent price hike might have cost them market share, but they were unsure of their market position since external factors had acted in the past year to depress the whole market. While they were relatively certain that marketing research was needed, the objectives of that research were very vague. Few action alternatives had been considered other than the possibility of rescinding the price hike. This was not very palatable to Hypothet marketing management since raw material cost increases had led them to plan for another price hike within the next six months.

Critical to the success of the Hypothet research project was the involvement of the marketing group in the design of the study. Not only were the implications for their business of specific research results clear to them, marketing management gained great insight into the real nature of their business problems through the exercises involved in developing attribute descriptions. We first set about structuring the alternative actions which were available to marketing. Next we laboriously developed a set of attributes which could be clearly communicated to the buyer and which had specific implications for selecting among alternative marketing tactics. In structuring alternative marketing actions, we determined that the most likely steps to be taken would be price hikes or reductions in those product attributes where the cost of the attribute did not compare favorably with the buyer's perceived value of that attribute. We selected six attributes which could be readily dealt with by subjects and which had definite business implications (Table 1).

TABLE 1

IMPORTANT
HYPOTHET OFFERING ATTRIBUTES

- PRODUCT QUALITY (PURITY)
- SPEED OF DELIVERY
- SYSTEM VS. PRODUCT SUPPLIER
- RATE OF PRODUCT INNOVATION FOR INDUSTRY
- PLANT PERSONNEL RETRAINING POLICIES
- SPEED OF TROUBLE-SHOOTING SERVICE

Given these attributes, we developed two levels for each one (Table 2). These were thought to be meaningful alternatives for subsequent tactical action in that maximum level corresponded to the level of performance currently attempted by Du Pont in its product offering while the lower levels corresponded to reasonable potential reductions.

TABLE 2

OFFERING TRADE-OFFS

ATTRIBUTE	HIGH LEVEL	LOW LEVEL
QUALITY	IMPURITIES LESS THAN ONE PART PER MILLION	IMPURITIES LESS THAN TEN PARTS PER MILLION
DELIVERY	WITHIN ONE WEEK	WITHIN TWO WEEKS
SYSTEM	SUPPLY TOTAL SYSTEM	SUPPLY CHEMICAL ONLY
INNOVATION	HIGH LEVEL OF R&D SUPPORT	LITTLE R&D SUPPORT
RETRAINING	RETRAIN ON REQUEST	TRAIN ON INITIAL PURCHASE
SERVICE	LOCALLY AVAILABLE	THROUGH HOME OFFICE

You may have noticed that up until now no mention has been made of the attribute, price. To study the methodological impact of different scaling methods, two ways of scaling

144

the attributes were used -- one which excluded price and one which involved a direct trade-off against price.

Roughly equal proportions of the 150 subjects interviewed were classified by job as:

- Purchasing
- Technical
- Administrative

Sampling was performed to insure that three customer classifications were represented in proportion to the actual marketplace. These classifications were:

- Primarily Du Pont Supplied
- Partially Du Pont Supplied
- Not Supplied by Du Pont

Each of the 150 respondents was asked both types of trade-off questions.

The dilemma which we faced in the attribute trade-off scaling procedure was how to represent all of the attributes at both levels without exceeding the information-processing capacity of the subject. Clearly, we could not give the subject an aural presentation of two product offerings differing on all six attributes and expect him to correctly understand it. However, we did want a realistic task which provided the same framework within which each preference measure would be obtained. Borrowing somewhat from Hughes' idea of the modified constant-sum scale we presented the subject with a description of an optimal hypothetical supplier and then offered him a pair-wise choice between two reductions in service. The text given the subject went something like this:

"Now suppose a hypothetical supplier offered the following:

- High level of product quality as evidenced by an average of less than one part impurities per million;

- Prompt delivery time with 95% of deliveries made within one week;

- Total supplier providing handling system as well as chemical;

- Continual development of innovative new products to serve the industry;

- Retraining of manufacturing personnel as needed by customers; and

- Troubleshooting capability available from technically trained local sales representatives."

As you can see, this description is composed of the most desirable of each of the two alternatives developed for each service attribute. The subject was then told:

"Now suppose the same hypothetical supplier was under pressure to raise prices, but sought instead to reduce costs by eliminating services which customers considered of little value, and that he had narrowed his choices down to two alternatives..."

At this point, two of the six possible reductions were described and the subject was asked:

"Which one of these reductions would you rather see?"

After obtaining an expression of preference for one of the two reductions, the subject was asked to indicate whether his preference for taking that reduction instead of the other was "strong," "moderate," or "weak." If the reply were "strong," he was then asked whether his preference was "very strong" or "somewhat strong." Similarly, if he expressed a weak preference he was asked to state whether it was "very weak" or "somewhat weak." So we had added to a paired comparison preference measure a strength of preference measure on a five-point scale (ranging from "very weak" to "very strong"). This question sequence was asked of each subject for each of six different pairs of service reductions.

Note that we ask about only six of the 15 pairs which may be generated by combining the six different service reductions. We judged that, given the length of time each question required and the difficulty of the questions involved, six pairings were all we could reasonably expect a subject to handle without fatigue hampering performance. In order to accomplish the scaling desired without asking all 15 possible paired comparisons, we used the strength of preference measure as a very literal index of the distance between the two items on an underlying dimension of perceived value.

The computer system controlling the CRT's enabled us to select which one of five predetermined sets of six pairs would be presented to each subject for comparison (Table 3). For the purpose of illustration, let us represent the six trade-off

alternatives by the letters A through F. The computer randomized the order of presentation of the pairs to minimize
any effects of order bias, and further, it randomized which
item in each pair would be read first.

TABLE 3

Given the Selected Ordering:	Computer Randomizes: Pair Order	Item Order
A B	E F	F E
C D	A B	A B
E F	D E	E D
B C	B C	C B
D E	F A	F A
F A	C D	D C

For each subject, the scale values for the six reductions
were obtained by first considering Item A as the reference
point and laying out the other items in reference to it. Thus,
if B were preferred very strongly to A, and C were preferred
very weakly to B, then A would be at 0, B at +5 and C at +6,
and so on. Then this relative scaling was repeated with each
of the other reductions treated as the reference point and
finally the six different scales were added together to get
the composite scaling for that subject.

Averaging the scale values for each of the six attributes
across subjects produced the result shown in Fig. 1. Since we
did not include price, these scale values do not correspond to
monetary values. The scale units could have been transformed
into dollars and cents had we included one or two price increase alternatives in the trade-off set. We chose, instead,
to conduct a separate trade-off analysis to assess price relationships.

It is clear that the proposed reductions in quality and
in product innovation were the least desirable by a wide mar-
gin. On the other hand, reductions in delivery and in plant
personnel retraining were the lease undesirable.

The finding that product quality and innovation were of
primary importance was rather expected but the moderately
high value buyers placed on supplying a total system was quite
surprising. A program to phase out selling the system

147

components had been under consideration by Hypothet marketing and had received moderate support. At the same time, some very costly outlays for warehousing had been made recently to reduce delivery to five days in regions of the country remote from manufacturing sites. The relatively low value of that attribute had significant implications for future warehousing commitments.

The differences in scaling patterns for the three job classifications were not as large as had been expected, but were in the anticipated direction (Fig. 2). Purchasing Department representatives saw the R&D effort manifested in continual product innovation as much less valuable than did administrative and technical personnel. Technical personnel, on the other hand, valued the total system capability of a supplier less than administrative or purchasing representatives.

FIGURE 1

RELATIVE RELUCTANCE TO DROP SUPPLIER SERVICES

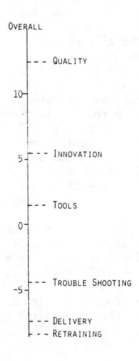

FIGURE 2

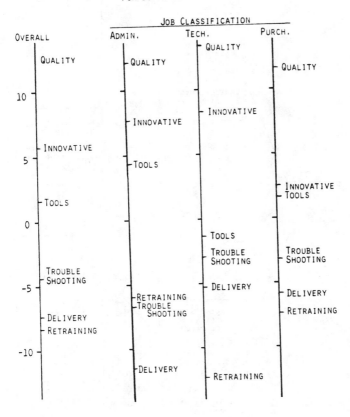

RELATIVE RELUCTANCE TO DROP SUPPLIER SERVICE
FOR DIFFERENT OCCUPATIONS

PRICE TRADE-OFFS

The second trade-off analysis involved a paired comparison of a price hike against a service reduction. Each subject was asked about only one service reduction because we felt respondent fatigue and systematic bias might affect the quality of the results. For example, those subjects who were asked about quality were asked to suppose that the hypothetical supplier had decided to take the action either of providing a chemical that offers fewer than ten parts per million instead of one part per million impurities, or of raising his price (Fig. 3).

FIGURE 3

DIRECT TRADE-OFF AGAINST PRICE

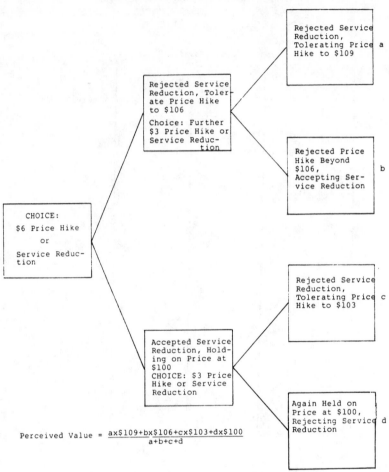

CHOICE:
$6 Price Hike
or
Service Reduction

Rejected Service Reduction, Tolerate Price Hike to $106

Choice: Further $3 Price Hike or Service Reduction

Rejected Service Reduction, Tolerating Price Hike to $109   a

Rejected Price Hike Beyond $106, Accepting Service Reduction   b

Accepted Service Reduction, Holding on Price at $100
CHOICE: $3 Price Hike or Service Reduction

Rejected Service Reduction, Tolerating Price Hike to $103   c

Again Held on Price at $100, Rejecting Service Reduction   d

$$\text{Perceived Value} = \frac{a \times \$109 + b \times \$106 + c \times \$103 + d \times \$100}{a+b+c+d}$$

"If not taking this action would mean that the supplier had to raise his price from $100 per unit to $106 per unit, would you choose to maintain the current program at the higher price or would you opt for holding on price and settling for ten parts per million impurities?"

150

If the subject chose to maintain the present quality standard, he was then asked how he would respond if the price were to be increased from $100 to $109. If he had first selected to hold on price he was asked secondly what his response would be if the price hike were to be only from $100 to $103.

The results of this second analysis, when compared with those of the first analysis (Fig. 4), reveal substantial agreement. The rank ordering is identical and the relative distances between the items on the two scales are quite similar. The correlation between the two scalings was .98. This level of agreement strengthened our confidence in the validity of our measurements

FIGURE 4

CUSTOMER RELUCTANCE TO DROP SUPPLIER SERVICES

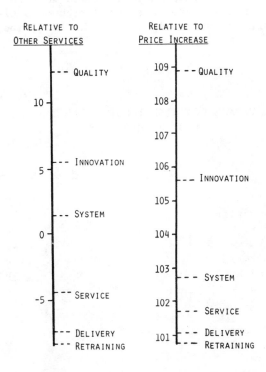

151

PERCEIVED VALUE OF SPECIFIC OFFERINGS

The subjects were also asked to evaluate the suppliers on each of these service attributes. The scale used here was the academic favorite ranging from "A" for excellent to "F" for failure or unacceptable. Earlier in the interview, we had asked subjects to indicate their familiarity with all major suppliers. The computer system running the CRT's prompted the interviewers to ask for attribute ratings only for those suppliers with which a subject had indicated familiarity. To speed up even further the interview, we had the program stop mentioning a given supplier if a subject indicated he did not know enough to rate a given company of the first two attributes.

These performance ratings on specific attributes, considered alone, were quite valuable to our client, but when they were combined with the preference data we were able to provide some especially useful information.

For example, with the perceived value of a given service expressed in monetary terms, we can speculate about the differential value of a given total product offering (Table 4). To derive the price premium contributions shown here, Du Pont's ratings as a supplier were contrasted with competitive ratings and the differences were weighted by the attribute utilities.

TABLE 4

AVERAGE CONTRIBUTIONS TO PRICE PREMIUM
OF EACH ATTRIBUTE

	DU PONT ADVANTAGE
Quality	$1.70
Innovation	2.00
System	.80
Service	.25
Delivery	.15
Retraining	.40
	$5.30

Base Price: $100

To do this we made two simplifying assumptions:

o that the supplier rating scale was an interval
  scale; and,

o that a rating of "A" on an attribute corresponded to the high level of that attribute
  while an "F" corresponded to the low level
  evaluated.

With these assumptions, we broke down the perceived
values of the attributes into intervals corresponding to the
differences between supplier ratings. For example, consider
the product quality attribute which had a perceived differential of $8.92. The difference between a supplier with an "A"
rating and one with a "B" rating would be $2.23. In a similar
manner, we can estimate the value of different hypothetical
product offerings representing specific service reductions
from the current Du Pont offering.

To summarize, we turned a request for a rather general
supplier-image study into a detailed and quantitative study.
Through involving the product marketing management in the
developmental stages of attribute selection and description,
we achieved credibility and acceptance of results even in
areas which were not favorable toward Du Pont. More importantly, though, we developed a piece of research which was
action-oriented and which resulted in specific marketing
activities, some of which were implemented immediately.
Keeping the project simple payed off substantially. The
rational nature of the buyer allowed us to simplify both the
stimulus presentation and the response task. The ease of
communicating the research methodology and findings to Hypothet marketing, sales and R&D made implementation of the
research conclusions much easier than it would have been with
a less understandable and, therefore, less credible methodology.

The result which most impressed me from the Hypothet
study was the degree of agreement between the direct scaling
procedure (the trade-off against price) and the indirect
scaling procedure (the trade-off between attribute pairs).
It appears to me that the industrial decision-maker can indeed
"read his own gauges," at least if the task is properly
defined.

DIRECT SCALING

I would like to show you the results of one more perceived

153

value study in which a direct scaling approach was used. I will refer to the Du pont product by the name "Supposit" to protect the identity of the actual product.

"Supposit" is an ingredient product which remains identified as a branded component of the final product manufactured by Du Pont's customers. "Supposit" marketing management requested marketing research because they were considering a certification of the performance of "Supposit" in the final product.

A few of Du Pont's larger customers were actively discouraging such a certification program since they perceived that it would reduce their competitive edge over smaller competitors.

The actual study was conducted with a self-administered questionnaire at a trade show but it could have been readily accomplished over the telephone. The methodology was similar to the "Dollarmetric" scaling proposed for consumer use by Meritt, Sharma and Woodside (1977) with one simplication. The procedure used here was modified so that instead of comparing product descriptions with each other pair wise, each of a set of 10 product descriptions was compared with a single standard product description. The standard product description simply gave a ficticious manufacturer name (Valpariso Co.) an unbranded ingredient description, and a below-average price, $6.25 per gallon. Valpariso Co. was identified as a small manufacturer, new in supplying this market. The use of a single standard stimulus was to reduce the information load placed on the subject.

Each subject was given the description of Valpariso's product and then told:

> "Please consider each of the alternatives on this sheet individually. For each one, I'd like you to mark the highest quote on that product which you would still accept over the Valpariso quote."

Each subject's questionnaire was computer-generated according to a predetermined randomization scheme which combined the names of ten end-product manufacturers with "Supposit," or a branded competitive product or an unbranded generic ingredient. Each subject was shown descriptions with all 10 manufacturers. Four of the 10 were paired with "Supposit," four with the competitive ingredient and two with the unbranded generic ingredient. For half of the subjects, "Supposit" appeared with the certification and without it for the other half.

Linear regression analysis of the data provided the desired measures of perceived value. One of the end-use manufacturers actually averaged less than the unknown comparison standard, Valpariso (Fig. 5). The premium associated with the name "Supposit" was measured with and without the proposed ingredient certification. "Supposit" was granted an $.18/gallon premium over the unbranded product, but its competitor received a $.30/gallon premium. However, when "Supposit" was combined with the certification, it was granted a $.39/gallon premium. Interestingly enough, the "Supposit" premium did not interact with manufacturer identification; rather it was fairly constant across manufacturers.

FIGURE 5

RELATIVE PERCEIVED VALUE OF
MANUFACTURER NAMES

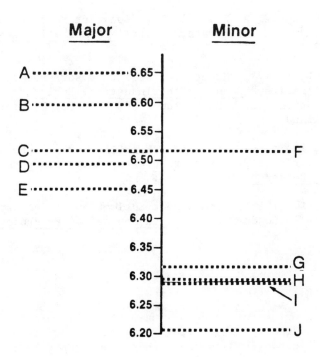

"Supposit" marketing management now has a means of evaluating the profit-to-cost ratio of implementing the certification program. Marketing research has another demonstration of the ease with which industrial buyers can provide direct estimates of the perceived value of product offering components.

I offer you these simple procedures for your own experimentation. In those cases where budget limitations, the narrow focus of the problem at hand, or other matters make conjoint measurement seem ill-advised, direct scaling of carefully developed attribute descriptions may offer you a means of retrieving utilities from industrial buyers without brain surgery or conjoint measurement.

REFERENCES

Ahtola, O. T. (1971), "The Vector Model of Preferences: An Alternative To the Fishbein Model," _Journal of Marketing Research_, 12, 52-59.

Bettman, J. R. (1979), "Memory Factors In Consumer Research: A Review," _Journal of Marketing_, 43, 37-53.

Green, P. E. and V. R. Rao (1971), "Conjoint Measurement for Quantifying Judgmental Data," _Journal of Marketing Research_, 18, 355-363.

Hughes, G. D. (1977), "Monetizing Utilities for Product and Service Benefits," _Consumer and Industrial Buying Behavior_, A. G. Woodside, J. N. Sheth and P. D. Bennett, New York: North Holland

Meritt, K., A. Sharma and A. G. Woodside (1977), "Dolpref: A Dollarmetric Program for Preference Analysis, _Journal of Marketing Research_, 14, 243-244.

Stevens, S. S. (1956), "The Direct Estimation of Sensory Magnitudes -- Loudness," _American Journal of Psychology_, 69, 1-25.

THE USE OF ATTITUDE RESEARCH -- WHAT'S HAPPENING AT THE FTC?

H. Keith Hunt, Brigham Young University, Provo

ABSTRACT

Attitude research and consumer research at the FTC is discussed. Particular attention is paid to copy tests as a type of attitude research seeing greatly increased use at the FTC. Specific FTC applications of attitude research are considered.

INTRODUCTION

Perhaps the single most important message I can give you today is that the use of consumer research at the FTC has changed. For several years you have heard the usual breast-beating presentation, usually by an academic, saying that the FTC really needed to use more consumer research in deciding which cases were worth the expenditure of public funds to pursue, in deciding what the key issues of a case would be, in the selection of research done by others to buttress the FTC position, and even in the ordering of new research to provide needed information. The change has occured more rapidly and to a greater extent than anyone ever thought possible.

I can still remember that when I joined the FTC staff in 1973 they were choking over an expenditure of, as I recall it, $30,000, to do a major piece of consumer research on a critical case. The previous high had been a few hundred dollars to pay out-of-pocket expenses for the ill-fated Wonder Bread study. Now, in 1979 and 1980, it is likely that the FTC will spend over a million dollars each year in budgeted research. Research to find out whether damages in the market are real and substantial is being done <u>before</u> cases are brought. Research for litigation is being done. Research on the probable effects of possible remedies is being done <u>before</u> the remedies are prescribed. Most of the things we had hoped for are being done. So we now find ourselves moving on from our early urgings that the FTC do more research to urging more careful attention to what kind of research the FTC had ought to be doing.

COGNITION MORE RELEVANT THAN ACTION TENDENCY OR AFFECT

There are many conceptualizations of attitude. I have always found the structural approach to be meaningful -- that is, that attitude consists of three interrelated components:

157

cognitions, affect, and action tendencies. This conceptualization is especially helpful in thinking about the material that
follows and is used as a base for the discussion.

As I have thought back over the FTC matters I am familiar
with, it struck me that in no case was the FTC primarily concerned about the affect component of attitude. Usually the FTC
is concerned with the cognitive component. And occasionally
the FTC is concerned with the action tendency component, but
even then it is often linked with attention to the cognitive
component. Why is there so little interest in affect?

One reason, I think, is the cultural value common in the
United States that individuals should be free to choose for
themselves what they will do. We abhor big brother telling us
what to do or exerting undue influence on us to behave in some
certain way. We feel individuals should be free to choose
except when that choice infringes on someone else's freedom to
choose. And we somehow have the opinion that we intrude less
on individual freedom of choice when we influence cognition than
when we influence affect or action tendency. Taking an example
so obvious as cigarettes, the product is admittedly dangerous
to the smoker's health. Yet we shy away from attempting to
regulate or legislate cigarettes out of existence. Instead we
provide information in an attempt to influence cognitions.
Then the cognitions are supposed to interact with affect and
action tendency, resulting in individuals decreasing or stopping
smoking. We are quite willing to go to great lengths to influence cognitions, but stay away from direct influence on
affect or on action tendency in public policy actions. For the
short time when the American Cancer Society was using negative
affect communications, smoking per capita actually declined.
But public policy efforts have stayed away from affect. For
another example, consider the problem of fetal alcohol syndrome
caused by heavy doses of alcohol taken by women within the first
couple of months of pregnancy. We as a society abhor the
thought of telling women who are potentially pregnant that they
can have only small doses of alcohol. And we would even oppose
a public campaign to try to get people to have negative affect
toward alcohol. But we are willing to engage in activities designed to influence individuals' cognitions about alcohol, attempting to develop a primarily negative cognitive loading toward alcohol use by potentially pregnant women.

Another specific value of those who influence FTC decisions
is that FTC activity should be restorative but not punitive. An
underlying assumption seems to be that by emphasizing cognition
rather than affect or action tendency, the FTC is less likely to
be punitive in its programs.

The result of these two values, (1) to maximize freedom of choice and freedom from government influence and (2) to be restorative rather than punitive, partially explains the emphasis of the FTC on monitoring and changing cognitions while paying little attention if not avoiding the other components of affect and action tendency. Actual FTC matters illustrate this point.

When I did my early work on corrective advertising effects, I reasoned that information influenced total beliefs, and that of the total set of beliefs or cognitions, there were a few which were salient or evaluative, and that those evaluative beliefs or cognitions led one to have some degree of positive or negative affect, which in turn influenced purchase intention, which in turn influenced purchase behavior. I reasoned that it would be unfruitful to expect a corrective statement regarding beliefs to **influence immediately** behavior. I even had my doubts about a corrective statement immediately influencing behavioral intention, although that was a possibility. I elected to use affect as my dependent measure because it was the step closest to purchase behavior likely to show immediate influence of a corrective statement. After substantial thinking about this and after extended discussions with Bill Wilkie, I changed to the view that the key dependent variable should be belief or cognition, not affect. If advertising needs correcting, what we need to correct are the beliefs, essentially the cognitions, which are incorrect. These _may_ have a substantial impact on affect and purchase intention, or they _may_ have _no_ impact at all on _either_ affect _or_ purchase intention. The advertiser's infraction was in creating a false belief, and the remedy should be the correction of that false belief. I suspect this thinking may change someday, but it shows no tendency to change yet.

The whole issue of corrective advertising centers on cognitions or beliefs, not on affect or action tendency. Deceptive or false advertising has created an incorrect set of cognitions. The problem is how to correct them. Just stopping the deceptive or false communications won't necessarily lead to a purging of the deceptive or false cognitions from the cognitive system. Rather, they may be firmly implanted and only information in direct conflict has any possibility of dislodging them. So the FTC and FDA send out corrective messages, either from the agency as with FDA or from the company itself, as with the FTC. Counteradvertising, an idea whose time has come and already gone again, also proposed that competitors or public interest groups could get involved in sending messages intended to correct the deceptive or false cognitions. The key issue here is belief or cognitions, not affect or action tendencies. The FTC has never, to my knowledge, attempted openly to change liking for a product or change behavioral intention for a product guilty of deceptive or false advertising. The most it has done is required efforts to correct the incorrect cognitions.

The carefully researched impact evaluation of the Listerine corrective advertising will give us insight into what impact on affect and action tendency a cognition correction might have. As it is ordered, the corrective message is purely cognitive in nature.

Recent investigation of the cognitions associated with life insurance also showed flawed cognitions. In New Jersey, life insurance companies are required to provide an informative booklet explaining key information regarding the actual cost of various policies from various companies. In a survey of consumers who had recently purchased insurance it was found that most consumers had no idea what they had bought, so the information program was not working -- the desired cognitions were not being developed. Also, the booklet and the salespeople were supposed to inform the consumer of the mandatory cooling off period, which it turns out most consumers did not understand, and those who thought they did understand it actually thought it was longer than it was, which is probably worse than having no awareness of it in the first place. Finally, to help consumers discriminate between high price policies and low price policies an indexing system was used, going from low to high, with low being the best buy and high being the worst buy, and consumers reversed the meaning and interpreted the high as the best buy and the low as the worst. With these serious gaps in understanding and misunderstandings of what was thought to be understood it is no wonder consumers were making poor choices in purchasing life insurance. The problem was with cognitions, not with affect or action tendencies.

Many recent FTC programs have focused on cognitions. I have just mentioned corrective advertising, which until now has been totally cognition oriented. Affirmative disclosure is also totally cognition oriented. The Hawaiian Punch type remedy requiring the inclusion of key information until marketer-caused incorrect cognitions have been corrected is totally cognition oriented. The funeral rule which has finally forced funeral directors to ally themselves with their kindred spirits, the used car dealers, in trying to avoid FTC regulation, was totally cognition oriented, asking the simple concession that funeral directors quote prices over the phone and for parts of the total funeral package rather than just a total price. If you go down the list of FTC activities, you find that almost all FTC matters are primarily, if not solely, cognition oriented. This is one of the key messages of this paper.

Just to support the adage that there is an exception to

every general statement, consider the recent STP corrective statement. That has been released but I haven't seen the copy, I've only heard about it. It was a pre/post design, with the pre-measure being taken before the public notice ads, and the post-measure being taken three weeks after the public notice ads started appearing. National telephone interviews were used. The sample consisted of general consumers and businessmen, with a third group included in the post measure -- advertising executives. Cognition was measured, and the business sample was more aware than the general public of the public notice ads. And the advertising executives were more aware than was the business sample. But what I am getting to is this, not only did cognition differ, but in this matter the evaluation also checked on purchase intention, and the general finding was that not only did people notice it but the message had a statistically significant impact on purchase intentions. While it wasn't clear whether the decline in purchase intentions was due to the publicity or the ads, both resulted from the FTC action, and purchase intention was signficantly negatively affected.

Also, the recent attention to the use of wood fibre in bread found that consumers had incorrect cognitions regarding the nature of the fibre. When the nature of the fibre was disclosed, it is reported that affect and action tendency were substantially affected.

What should be the case? I don't know. But it is evident that up to now the FTC has focused its interest on the cognitive component of attitude. I predict that we will see more attention to affect and to action tendencies. Some studies have already shown that cognitive corrections cause negative shifts in affect for the total firm. While these have been viewed as side effects up to now, that view will certainly change as more evidence is compiled showing the influence of cognitive corrections on both affect (toward the brand and the company) and behavioral intention (toward the brand and the company).

COPY TESTS

There really aren't very many advertising cases any more which are chosen for action which don't have some copy tests done first to look at beliefs and attitudes toward the advertising. It used to be that a couple of attorneys would sit around looking at ads, usually print ads, and find some that looked like they might be deceptive, and they would decide to take action against those ads.

A recent consent order in this area is the Fresh Horizons

Bread, the one using wood pulp to add fibre to bread. Several different copy tests were run on consumers' attitudes and perceptions before the matter became a formal investigation. To those of us who have worked in the area for years, the good news of this development is still hard to believe. After so many years of feeling we were braying in the wilderness, it is nothing short of amazing that such a rapid shift to the use of copy tests could occur.

And this use of attitude research, however loosely defined, shows increasingly sophisticated use. As the researchers from the business and academic attitude research community have gone inside the FTC and other agencies, the previous naivete within the agencies has disappeared and we find agency personnel, us on the inside, asking the "right" questions for a change -- right from a professional point of view -- rather than the legal questions the attorneys have been asking over the years. The result is that attitude research is now used by people who are well schooled in the area rather than by attorneys who learned just enough about attitude research to get them through the one case. John Eighmey had a great impact, being in a management position at the FTC and having strong influence on what the attorneys under him were doing regarding attitude research. More intelligent research was commissioned from experts in the field. And Ken Bernhardt had a major impact in getting the impact evaluation research work going.

While copy tests conducted by a firm in its normal advertising activities may not be ideal for litigation, they can show more than simply deception or misperception. Suppose a situation where a company's copy tests for a product have been subpoened, and they show a pattern that in the early days of a product's existence no questions were asked about the allegedly deceptive claim, but the essence of the deceptive claim showed up in the verbatims. On the next year's copy tests the verbatims were coded to account for the deceptive claim. And in the succeeding years the number of mentions of that deceptive claim increase. Here the FTC has a clear picture of a claim which might not have originally been intended to be deceptive, but which, when it was discovered to be deceptive in the favor of the firm, was enhanced and embellished to further its selling power. Such a finding, should it occur, would provide an interesting use of copy research.

SPECIFIC APPLICATIONS OF ATTITUDE RESEARCH

Finally, I'd like to discuss some specific applications of attitude research at the FTC.

162

Performance Remedies

It is no secret that the FTC is doing several studies which would fit under the category of attitude research involving Listerine. After the analgesic cases come through the final pipeline it appears that in several there will be corrective advertising. It appears that corrective advertising will be an increasingly important remedy. And attitude research will be part of that remedy in the form of performance remedies. What is a performance remedy? Usually a corrective advertising remedy has said that a certain amount of advertising has to carry the corrective message. The FTC specifies the content of the message and the time or dollar volume of advertising for which the corrective advertising has to be included. There is some evidence the FTC is getting away from this standard procedure and moving toward what has come to be called performance remedies. Instead of prescribing a specified amount of corrective advertising, the FTC shows the amount of deception and specifies an acceptable level for that measure and leaves it up to the company to reduce the incorrect perception to the specified level. The first of this type of remedy was the Hawaiian Punch remedy in which Hawaiian Punch was required to carry an affirmative disclosure of the amount of natural fruit juice contained in Hawaiian Punch until it could show that specified percentages of consumers correctly understood the natural fruit juice content in Hawaiian Punch. The remedy was ineffective because Hawaiian Punch embedded the affirmative disclosure in the total information on the label and in the ads so it did not detract in any way from the general message. No effort was ever made to achieve the performance standard specified by the FTC because the affirmative disclosure had no impact. However, recent performance standards have been more carefully designed. For example, in the AMF consent order on bicycle safety, AMF was required to distribute public service announcements on bicycle safety to a specified number of stations. If the prescribed number of the stations run the PSA's that satisfies the performance remedy. If an insufficient number run the spots, then the PSA's have to be sent out to additional stations, and so on, until the required number of stations have run the PSA's. The goal, of course, is message exposure. The same thing will be done with the components of consumer attitudes. Incorrect cognitions caused by the deceptive ad will have to be corrected to a specified level or dire consequences will be imposed by the FTC. But the way the deceptions are corrected will be up to the advertiser within quite broad limits. Just so you keep your history straight, the original Hawaiian Punch remedy was primarily the thinking of Bill Wilkie as he struggled to find some better approach than requiring a percentage of advertising or specified time period for running the corrective ad consisting of FTC prescribed copy.

Problem Documentation

Another use of attitude research is developing rapidly at the FTC. There is increasing use of research to document and examine problems proposed for FTC action before the FTC jumps in to launch an investigation or propose some remedy. The best example of this type of remedy at this time is the study of housing defects. Most of us have known for a long time that there is a problem with defects in housing. But is the problem one requiring FTC action? The FTC knows consumers are getting ripped off because they get lots of complaint letters. But the question remains as to whether all consumers find defects, and whether these defects are the functions of being in a new building before all the bugs are worked out, or whether builders are doing less than adequate quality building, thus causing the defects. And, if the defects are widespread, what kinds of remedies might clear up the situation. While the housing defects matter isn't so much attitude research, it is easy to see that on some future problem, attitude research could be the key issue. Some who have been on the FTC staff are generally of the opinion that there are several matters in the past which would never have seen the light of day had the FTC done some problem documentation research before the matter went too far.

Prospective Studies

Often called strategy evaluations, prospective (pro as in grow) studies attempt to assess the likely outcomes if different remedies are used. Usually there are several alternative remedies. The public policy question is which remedy or set of remedies should be used to accomplish the policy objectives.

Often associated with prospective studies is the matter of at-risk consumers. Sometimes an FTC matter will be a concern not to all consumers but to only certain consumers having characteristics which make certain products or practices a risk to them when the same products or practices are not a risk to general consumers. The ideal remedy is one which brings about the change in attitude and/or behavior in the at-risk consumers while having no influence on the not-at-risk consumer. But often the warning could scare people it didn't apply to. Or the corrective message could lead to misperception in people not deceived by the original problem ad. It's an empirical question. And we will see more and more use of attitude and other research to evaluate which of several remedies will effectively accomplish the objectives without having negative effects on those consumers who have no relevant concern with the matter.

Joint Research

Most FTC attitude research is done in an advocacy setting, with each side trying to find secondary research or do primary research which will support its side of the matter. About four years ago Bill Wilkie and I worked for the FTC on a matter in which there was a point of substantial disagreement between two sides. Yamaha had made a statement in an ad that with proper instruction a motorcycle could be just as safe as a car. An FTC attorney somewhat experienced with motorcycles and their safety took exception to the statement and took the FTC into litigation against Yamaha and its advertising agency. The key issue in the matter was how consumers perceived that statement. And that was an empirical question. The two sides decided to proceed with a simple research study to find out how consumers perceived the message. A non-binding pilot of the study was tested, and the results were so powerful that the matter was settled with a consent decree. What I found so interesting in this matter is that both sides were saved tremendous litigation costs through the simple step of asking the empirical question at the heart of the matter. And it was done jointly, with both parties agreeing to the design of the study and the actual study being done by a third party. As far as I know, this only happened once. It's interesting that the researchers involved came away with the highest professional regard for each other.

Differences Between FTC Research and Company Research

I had intended to give an extensive discussion of the differences between research done for management decision making and research done for public policy or litigation matters. But in reviewing all the papers at my disposal I found that Ken Bernhardt already did that. And after carefully reviewing his material I found I had nothing to add. So let me simply refer you to Bernhardt's (in press) paper presented at the American Marketing Association workshop on "Exploring and Developing Government Marketing," presented May 3-4, 1979, and available from him until the proceedings of the conference come out.

SUMMARY

So there it is. Attitude research is being used more than we ever thought it would be used at the FTC. It seems that cognitions are the primary component relevant to FTC decisions, although there is slight interest evident in affect and in action tendencies. Copy testing has become an established fact at the Commission. And performance remedies, problem documentation, prospective studies of remedies, effective for at-risk consumers, and joint venture research are ideas that to varying degrees are coming of age at the FTC. Whatever else may be said at this time, we can end this discussion by repeating that attitude research is being used more than any of us ever thought possible at the FTC, and all indications are that that use will continue to increase.

A MANAGERIAL PERSPECTIVE ON
SEGMENTATION RESEARCH

Tyzoon T. Tyebjee, University of Santa Clara, Santa Clara

ABSTRACT

The paper develops a framework for evaluating market segmentation research in an applied setting. Six evaluation factors are proposed, namely the homogeneity, validity, stability, accessibility and profitability of the segments, and the
overall relevance of the segmentation scheme to managerial decision-making.

INTRODUCTION

The concept of market segmentation is pervasive in modern
marketing thought and practice. The literature on market segmentation has largely concerned itself with the strategic benefits of market segmentation, and the operational issues of
which characteristics of consumers or brands and which multivariate analyses are appropriate for market segmentation.
There has been little attention paid to the equally important
issue concerning the effectiveness of a particular segmentation
scheme for managerial purposes. To the extent that markets can
be segmented in many different ways, each resulting segmentation scheme may not be equally valuable to a manager in any
given context. In this paper, a model for evaluating a segmentation scheme is proposed.

The model consists of six factors on which segments can
be evaluated. The six factors and the questions which arise
from them, are:

Factor	The Question
1) Homogeneity	Are consumers in the same segment similar to each other and different from those in other segments?
2) Validity	Does the partitioning of the market into segments reflect natural groupings to be found in reality? Do the segments show differences in behavior?
3) Stability	Are the number, size and nature of segments sufficiently stable over a

166

period of time long enough for planning purposes?

4) Accessibility   Can different marketing strategies
be selectively targeted to each seg-
ment?

5) Profitability   Are the segments sufficiently large
to be profitable?

6) Managerial Goals   Does the segmentation scheme fulfill
the managerial goals for which it is
intended?

Each of these factors are discussed in the subsequent sec-
tions.

HOMOGENEITY OF SEGMENTS

The essence of market segmentation is to partition the
market into homogeneous subgroups. Thus it is crucial that a
segmentation scheme result in homogeneous market segments.
Segments need to be evaluated for homogeneity in the segmentation criteria by which they are defined, and also other relevant criteria useful in describing the segments.

When empirical methods such as cluster analysis are used
to segment the market, the result achieved is rarely a perfect
partitioning. Empirically derived segments may demonstrate a
considerable amount of overlap in their distributions of the
criteria used to generate segments. To better grasp the problem of homogeneity, we can consider a hypothetical distribution
of preferred level of an attribute, say styling, as shown in
Figure 1.

FIGURE 1

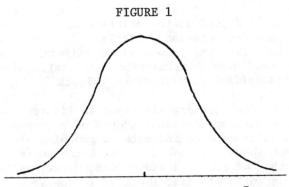

Degree of Styling

If this distribution had been subjected to cluster analysis to generate three homogeneous subgroups, the distribution of the styling preferences of the resulting subgroups may be as shown in Figure 2.

FIGURE 2

Group 2

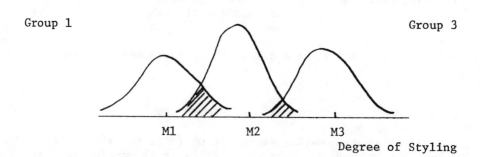

Group 1

Group 3

M1   M2   M3

Degree of Styling

Clearly, there is a considerable degree of overlap in the subgroups. This overlap mars our ability conceptually to treat the subgroups as distinct in the degree of styling preferred, even though the mean of each group M1, M2, and M3 show a clear separation. This points to the well known fact that the differences in groups' means should be viewed in temperance with the variability within each group. Even large differences between group means may not signify very much if the within-group variability is very large.

The appropriateness of empirical clustering methods for a particular set of data can be decided on statistical grounds. Empirical clustering methods, after all, search the data for "natural" groupings of similar people. The ability to find such groupings will depend to what extent they are present, which in turn will depend on the statistical distribution of the scores on the segmentation criteria. The simple case of two segmentation criteria, namely price and style consciousness, will be used here to illustrate graphically three extreme examples of statistical distributions (Figure 3).

Each dot in the scattergrams shown in Figure 3 represents the price and style consciousness scores of a consumer. Areas with a high density of dots indicate a grouping of consumers. The first graph shows a set of data where consumers are highly dispersed on the two criteria and no concentrations exist; that is, the data is <u>uniformly distributed</u>. In the second graph,

FIGURE 3

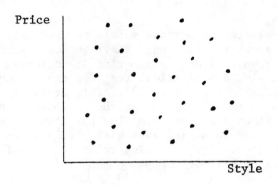

Uniform Distribution

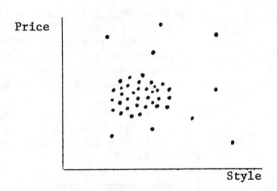

Uni-modal Distribution

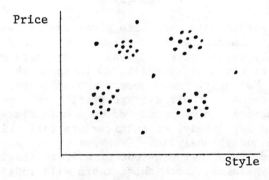

Multi-modal Distribution

there is one region in which there is a disproportionate number of people, indicating one mode or one "natural" grouping. This is called a uni-modal distribution. The third group shows several groupings or clusters, and is called a multi-modal distribution.

Empirical clustering methods should be used only when one has data which show a multi-modal distribution. When several criteria are present, visual examination is no longer sufficient. Fortunately, a statistical test for the presence of clusters is available (Arnold 1979). This statistic allows the researchers to identify which of the above three distributions best describes a set of data. The partitioning method which should be used on a data base will partly depend on the type of distribution. The following rules can help in selecting the appropriate method.

Type of Distribution	Appropriate Partitioning Method
1) Uniform	Use a priori judgments to establish cutoffs on each of the criteria, if the spread on each criterion warrants segmentation. Otherwise, treat the market as non-segmentable, or look for other criteria to segment on.
2) Uni-modal	There is only a single homogeneous group. Treat the market as non-segmentable, or develop new segmentation criteria.
3) Multi-modal	Several natural groupings are present. Use empirical clustering methods to find these groupings and segment accordingly.

After the partitioning has been completed, a post-hoc analysis of the segments can be checked to see whether the desired homogeneity was achieved. Ideally, consumers within a segment should be close to identical in terms of the segmentation criteria. Moreover, the segments should demonstrate clear differences in terms of their average profile on these criteria. This evaluation can be conducted by a univariate (each criterion tested separately) or multivariate (all criteria tested simultaneously) analysis. The appropriate statistical tests to be used are either a t-test of differences in mean or an analysis of variance. Both these tests will indicate the extent to which the differences in the segments are diluted by a lack of homogeneity within each segment.

The source of any lack of homogeneity can be located by:

a) Identifying which segmentation criteria are responsible for overlapping segments. A univariate t-test is the simplest procedure to accomplish this step.

b) Identifying which segments overlap to a great degree. The degree of overlap can be represented by a statistic known as the Mahanolobis distance.

If the segments derived lack homogeneity on a particular segmentation criterion, this criterion is a candidate for deletion. If two segments are very "close" as judged by the Mahalanobis distance, these segments are candidates to be merged.

The importance of evaluating segments for homogeneity of segmentation criteria and other managerially relevant characteristics bears repetition. Market segmentation is not simply a partitioning of a market. It is the partitioning of a market into groups whose members are similar to each other on one or more managerially relevant characteristics. In partitioning the market, the use of the appropriate partitioning method will improve the ability to identify homogeneous groups. Once the groups are established, it is worthwhile to use some of the tests described in this segment to evaluate to what extent homogeneity has been achieved.

VALIDITY OF SEGMENTS

A market segmentation scheme must be valid. Validity is one of the most complex issues of social science research. For our purposes, the validity of a segmentation scheme can be taken to mean the extent to which the "view of the world" inferred from a particular analysis on a particular set of data collected from a particular sample, in fact, reflects reality. (For a discussion of validity, reliability and stability of market segments, see Wells (1975) and Wind (1978)).

The importance of validity needs little amplification. Management's interest in the results of segmentation research stems from a desire to gain a better understanding of its market(s). If the results of the research were invalid, any understanding gained from them would be deceptive about the realities of the market.

The validity of segmentation research can be enhanced by the careful design of the sample and the questionnaire, so as to ensure projectability of the sample and the confidence in the measures obtained. The segmentation criteria used must be related to the behavior which the manager wishes to influence, and the analysis of these criteria must use techniques which are compatible with the limitations of the data. Thus validity must be of foremost concern throughout the research process. In this section we will discuss additional tests which can be conducted to evaluate to what extent the desire for validity has been achieved once the research has been completed.

There are two types of validity, namely, internal and external validity. <u>Internal validity</u> examines additional relationships in the same sample. <u>External validity</u> examines the relationship between the results of the segmentation research derived from a set of data to what one actually observes in the market.

Internal Validity

Additional analyses of the segmentation research data can validate the segmentation scheme. Two types of analyses are possible. One set of analyses inquires as to how well the segmentation criteria predict membership in the correct segment. To evaluate this, each segment's members are split into subsamples, the estimation sample and the validation sample. The estimation sample from all segments is input to a discriminant analysis which builds a mathematical rule by which the segment membership of the persons in the estimation sample is best predicted. The same mathematical rule is then used to predict the segment membership of each person in the validation sample. The percentage of the validation sample whose segment membership is accurately predicted by the mathematical function derived on the basis of the estimation sample is an index of the ability of segmentation criteria to classify consumers in their actual segments.

A second check on internal validity is the relationship between segments and purchase behavior. If the segments have been defined in terms of criteria other than purchase behavior, it becomes important to identify how much the segments differ in their purchase behavior. The managerial value of segmentation schemes, however much the segments meet the homogeneity criteria, is reduced if the segments show no differences in the purchase behavior which the manager wishes to influence. These checks on behavioral differences can be evaluated by a series of questions and tests about the purchase behavior of each segment.

Question	Statistical Analysis
Is the average purchase volume of segments different?	T-test for differences in group means of purchase volume.

172

Is the difference in purchase volume between segments greater than the difference between persons in the same segment?	Analysis of variances in purchase volume across segments.
Is the favorite brand of each segment different?	Chi-square test on the frequency of each brand as purchased by each segment.
How well do segmentation criteria predict purchase volume?	A regression analysis using the segmentation criteria as independent variables and the purchase volume as the dependent variable. (For some caveats in such use of regression, see Bass, Tigert and Lonsdale (1968) and Morrison (1973)).

External Validity

The results drawn from a set of data can be applied to the market as a whole only to the extent that the results have external validity. External validity can be evaluated by examining the predictability of the sample. Are all groups of consumers (e.g., by sex, geographic area, occupation, etc.) represented in the sample in the same proportion as in the marketplace? To the extent that the sample data allow predictions about brand share and product category purchase statistics, how well do these predictions match up with what is known about the market? Finally, are the results of the segmentation research data consistent with other data bases of the same market, e.g., diary panels, store auditors, etc.? These are questions to be asked of the segmentation research before extending its results to decisions which affect the marketplace.

STABILITY OF SEGMENTS

For a manager to base decisions on a segmentation scheme, there must be some confidence that the segments derived are stable, and not the happenstance of a particular data base at a particular point in time. Stability implies that if the research were replicated, the results would be essentially the same over a period of time long enough to allow management to develop strategies for a planning horizon.

Two types of replication are possible to evaluate stability. The first is to repeat the research on the same sample at two different times. This is similar to the notion of test-retest reliability. This type of replication is relatively uncommon because it is often prohibitively expensive. Also, there is always the danger that once a sample has been interviewed, the research process itself changes the character of the sample and introduces a bias in the second wave interview.

One study of benefit segmentation of bank customers found that the analysis of two waves of data on the same sample resulted in essentially the same segmentation scheme as judged by the number, profile and size of segments and derived at each point in time (Calantone and Sawyer 1978). However, the study did find that individual consumers showed poor stability in that the same consumer was likely to be in different segments over the two year period of study. Seventy percent of the sample had changed from one segment to another during the two years. Thus this study of replicated segmentation research indicates that segments are more stable in their aggregate character than at the more micro-level of exactly which individuals belong to which segment.

A second approach to assessing stability is to conduct the same analyses on two separate samples drawn from the same sample frame. This can be achieved by taking any sample and randomly dividing it into two parts or by drawing two independent samples at two different points in time.

The results of the analyses based on the two independent samples should be similar if the segments are to be stable. The same number segments with the same relative sizes and the same profile should result from both samples. One study of lifestyles, using independent samples, found that the psychographic profiles of segments, defined a priori in terms of brand bought, were highly comparable for each segment across the two samples (Kinnear and Taylor 1976). However, when segments were developed by cluster analyses of the pscyhographic measures the number, size and profile of the segments were different for the two samples and, also, very sensitive to the clustering technique used.

The published evidence on stability is scant. Therefore, it is impossible to generalize the extent to which researchers need to worry about the volatility of their segmentation schemes. A prudent approach would be to evaluate the segmentation approach for its stability over time. A direct implication of this recommendation is that segmentation research should not be static but rather provide a continuous monitor on the dynamics of the market.

ACCESSIBILITY OF SEGMENTS

If different strategies are to be targeted for different segments, the ability of a firm to selectively reach each segment becomes important in evaluating a segmentation scheme. For example, if segments have been defined in terms of price-quality preferences, and there were no relationship between this partitioning and marketing access variables, such as kind of media or stores used, the only way that different price strategies could be implemented would be by a shotgun approach. Each price-quality line would have to be advertised and distributed to each person regardless of the segment, since no media or channels exist to access selectively each segment. This shotgun approach is less cost-effective than a rifle approach where selective access to each segment is possible.

A simple way to evaluate the segmentation scheme in terms of selective accessiblity is to cross-tabulate the segment against marketing access variables such as media usage, store patronage, and geographic location (Table 1).

TABLE 1

ACCESS VEHICLE

		A_1	A_2	A_3	A_4	A_5
S E G M E N T S	S_1					
	S_2					
	S_3					
	S_4					

The entry in each cell, R_{ij}, of the above matrix, should measure the percentage of segment S_i reached by the access vehicle A_j. To evaluate the segmentation scheme, each column should be scanned. If for each segment, one or more access vehicles can be found such that they together reach a high proportion of that segment but not other segments, the selective accessibility can be established. Of course, if the vehicles which allow selective access are cost-prohibitive, it may be preferable to replace them with less selective vehicles which are more cost-efficient. If selectivity is sacrificed for reasons of cost-efficiency in access, it should be done only after the effect of reaching a segment with several strategies is considered.

175

PROFITABILITY OF SEGMENTS

The purpose of any segmentation is to identify sub-markets. Each segment becomes the focus of a different strategy, and often requires a separate organizational infrastructure. In evaluating the profitability of a segment the essential question is whether the profits from that segment warrant the additional costs imposed by a distinct strategy and organization.

The profitability of a segment will depend, of course, on the revenue and costs associated with the appropriate strategy designed for the segment. These, in turn, will depend on:

a)   The number of persons in the segment

b)   The product quality and features required by the segment

c)   The promotion costs in reaching and stimulating the segment

d)   The channel costs of distributing to the segment

Once the profits associated with each segment are established, management may choose to ignore those segments with less than acceptable profitability. Alternatively, these segments can be merged by examining their relative similarity to yield large segments. The evaluation of a segmentation scheme in terms of profit impact reduces the danger of oversegmenting the market.

The stages in the product's life cycle should also be considered in evaluating whether a market has been overly segmented. Often, when a product is in the maturity stage, the market for that product tends to be highly fragmented as several competitors vie to increase market share in a non-growth market. For this reason, in the maturity stage, competitive pressure may force a firm to segment a market into more groups than economic considerations warrant. This situation, however, does not continue indefinitely as the economics of such fragmented markets usually results in a shake-out, that is, the exit of marginal competitors. Naturally, the ability to survive a shake-out is critical in oversegmented or fragmented markets.

RELEVANCE TO MANAGERIAL GOALS

Management undertakes segmentation research with implicit or explicit expectations that the results of the research will foster better decisions. Depending upon the decisions which the research is expected to provide inputs, certain segmentation criteria have proved more appropriate than others. A state of the art review of market segmentation literature reports six areas of managerial concern where market segmentation research is relevant (Wind 1978). These six managerial goals for segmentation research are tabulated below, and for each goal the segmentation criteria which are most appropriate are listed.

Managerial Goal	Segmentation Criteria
1. General understanding of the market	Benefits sought Product purchases and usage patterns Needs Brand loyalty and switching
2. Product positioning	Product usage Product preference Benefits sought
3. New product development	New concept preferences and intention to buy Benefits sought
4. Pricing decisions	Price sensitivity Deal proneness Price sensitivity by purchase/ usage patterns
5. Advertising decisions	Benefits sought Media usage Psychographic and life-style Purchase and usage patterns
6. Distribution decisions	Store loyalty and patronage Benefits sought in store selection

Once the market has been partitioned into segments, the variables which effectively define the segments must be those which are useful for the decisions facing management. For example, segments defined in terms of psychographic profiles may be very useful in developing advertising copy, but may be virtually useless for pricing products for each segment. For the pricing decisions, the segments would also have to show differences in price sensitivity.

Finally, in firms where the segmentation research tasks and functions are performed at a locus which is organization-

177

ally distinct from the managers who are responsible for designing and implementing strategies directed towards the segments, it is crucial that the segmentation research survive the
researcher-to-manager interface. Management's acceptance of
segmentation research results as relevant to its needs will
be improved if:

a) The manager has been continually involved at all phases of
    the segmentation research design, execution and analysis.

b) The assumptions and limitations of the research data and
    analysis are understood by managers.

c) The research results are easily communicated in managerial,
    as opposed to technical, language.

d) The results are compatible with the wealth of experience
    managers bring to a decision situation.

e) The impact of the research is evolutionary rather than
    revolutionary.

f) The implications of the research can be implemented on a
    trial basis so as to reduce the economic risk for the firm
    and the professional risk for the manager.

SUMMARY

Consumers and brands in any market can be described in
terms of a wide variety of characteristics. Each of these
characteristics, either in itself or in combination with
others, is a potential basis for segmenting the market. To
the extent that there is no one unique way of segmenting the
market, a manager must decide which of several competing segmentation schemes is viable in a particular managerial situation. This paper has developed a systematic approach for a
managerial evaluation of a segmentation scheme on several factors. Such an evaluation would allow a manager to identify
the strengths and weaknesses of segmentation schemes for the
purposes of marketing decisions.

REFERENCES

Arnold, S.A. (1979), "A Test for Clusters," Journal of Marketing Research 16 (November), 545-51.

Bass, F.M., D.J. Tigert, and D.T. Lonsdale (1968), "Market Segmentation: Group Versus Individual Behavior," Journal of

Marketing Research, 5 (August), 264-70.

Calantone, R. J. and A. G. Sawyer (1978), "The Stability of Benefit Segments," Journal of Marketing Research, 15 (August), 395-404.

Kinnear, T. C. and J. R. Taylor (1976), "Psychographics: Some Additional Findings," Journal of Marketing Research, 13 (November), 422-25.

Morrison, D. G. (1973), "Evaluating Market Segmentation Studies: The Properties of R^2," Management Science, 19 (July), 1213-21.

Wind, Y. (1978), "Issues and Advances in Segmentation Research," Journal of Marketing Research, 15 (August), 317-37.

Wells, W. D. (1975), "Psychographics: A Critical Review," Journal of Marketing Research, 12 (May), 196-212.

ATTITUDE RESEARCH ENTERS THE FINANCIAL WORLD

Walter B. Kirkman, Chase Manhattan Bank, New York

ABSTRACT

This paper emphasizes the applications of attitudinal research as a basis for marketing action in the banking world.
At least, insofar as that portion of the banking world is
exemplified by our actions at the Chase Manhattan Bank.

Over the past decade, and especially since 1974, we have
seen banking move swiftly from a place one goes to store money,
borrow money, and process financial transactions, to a place
that now provides a significant number of other financial
services. As inflationary pressures build, and other non-
banking organizations assume quasi-banking and financial roles
the increased competitiveness of the market has required banks
to undertake significant changes. Some examples of these
changes are to employ more sophisticated hardware and software,
apply new technology to meet the critical needs of speed in
areas of banking ranging from global transactions to personal
transactions at an automatic teller machine, and to add new
convenient product services such as bank by phone, NOW accounts,
automatic lines of credit, debit cards, etc. These competitive
pressures have precipitated revised organizational requirements
as well, and, as a part of this, much more sophisticated
marketing. In fact, whole areas of the business of a bank
have been reconfigured--i.e., into marketing groups such as
discrete segments of business, categories of banking services
which we call lines of business, and in the retail, or consumer
areas, into segments of market. And that fact, those events
brought about so recently really set the stage for my talk
today.

Attitudinal research is relatively new in banking circles
and in my bank, as well. Eight years or so is the approximate
time frame wherein development of attitudinal research methods
have earned a place in bank marketing. But it has been only
in the past four or five years where the methodologies have
begun to be pursued vigorously and actively applied. Measurements stemming from attitudinal research of one sort or the
other are in active use in the principal wholesale banking
areas nationally and internationally, and in retail banking.
It is in this latter area wherein we find the most advanced
utilization of attitudinal research at Chase, today.

I plan to describe in general terms the applications of
attitudinal research in wholesale banking and then share with

you a marketing program under development based upon a recent attitudinal research study in our Retail Bank.

First, some comments about the wholesale banking area. By way of distinguishing one area from the other, and broadly speaking, wholesale banking includes the following: Corporate bank involves lending to major national and multi-nationals, Institutional banking--inter-bank servicing for international and domestic correspondent banks and other financial institutions, and loan and non-loan functions directly associated with International banking. In these areas a bank's competitive position depends, in the main, upon the business conditions, past experience with the bank, skills in operations, negotiating position and, importantly, interpersonal attitudes that prevail at all levels within a given company relative to that bank.

Chase, and most other major banks in the U.S. have been measuring attitudes about their bank, their people, along with that of their principal competitors both in the U.S. and in selected countries abroad for a number of years. One of the most important groups of these are the attitudes held by key corporate customers regarding the relationship manager, or bank's calling officer. As a case in point, three years ago measurements of customer attitudes about Chase's calling officers showed this critical functional area at the bank to be deficient compared with two key competitors.

The most significant attributes for improvement were determined to be these:

· follow up--promptly and effectively
· knowledge of a company's needs & of their industry
· makes meaningful use of time when visiting
· able to confine the bank to meet credit requirements
· limit calling officer turnover

As the result of a coordinated program to address this issue, one which includes pointed sales training, improved internal procedures, and advertising addressed specifically to these attributes, improved dramatically. These same attitudinal measurements now show the Bank to be regarded in a premier position for the principal and the lead bank designation, the key target customers. And that has been accomplished over a two year time frame.

The information analyzed from these continuing studies have been especially helpful in pointing up the trends in each of many other perceptions about our bank and competition, and in stimulating careful consideration of those changes that can be made to improve the bank's position competitively. By that

we mean, overcome perceived deficiencies, communicate our
strengths and to emphasize internally those skills which are
deemed to be not only relevant to the banking relationship but
critical to establish a preferential position for Chase.

In summary regarding wholesale banking, we find the corporate customer, the multi-national customer, the correspondent
banker and those relationships in other large organizations
involved with banking do respond in an attitudinal sense,
perceptions can be changed, behavior internally and amongst
our key customers has improved. And we are dealing with
diverse management functions at various decision levels within
corporations that have differing needs, and hold vastly
different attitudes about the banks they deal with. Understanding their different needs and their attitudes about your
bank's products, services, procedures, perceived banking skills,
senior management, etc. can make a difference in the effectiveness of the overall marketing efforts and the impact of the
communications programs.

Now lets move from the brief trip through global banking
to consumer banking. In doing so think about banking in a
single metropolitan area—principally the five boroughs comprising New York City plus surrounding counties. Conceive of
your normal branch bank, and Chase has about 200 of these in
New York Metro—and, in this instance, individual neighborhoods
as the scope of the marketing universe. And change the audience
target—from the various levels of corporate financial managers,
to a full range of our citizenry as private individuals.

Although a mass market, as far as Chase is concerned, a
mass marketing approach to the N.Y. metropolitan market is
not desirable for a number of reasons.

1. The situation that exists by virtue of competitive marketing
   efforts.

   --confusion concerning banking
   · due to the changes in rates, services
   · economic uncertainty

   --too many "general" messages
   · collectively talking about too many little understood
     services
   · too much communication over kill or information overload

2. Among consumers, the incidence of bank switching is not that
   prevalent, yet new household units and individuals with
   multiple accounts and users of multiple services are very
   important to growth and to profit.

182

3. Typical to service industries there is a wide variance possible in the quality of the overall delivery system from competitive bank to bank, and within a single bank from branch to branch.

4. And finally, the demography of individual neighborhoods differ significantly within the New York Metro and continues to change and thus the attitudes towards the various financial services will differ, as well.

The strategic direction decided upon by Chase marketing management was to establish a marketing program based on the individual family unit whose personal attitudes and skills would classify them as strivers and economically as upwardly mobile. You will notice that this is a strategy based upon attitudes, as well as economic and demographic factors.

The objective of a recent attitudinal segmentation study was to determine whether we could segment the market based upon attitudes, behavior, economics and demographics so as to address collectively current retail customer's banking needs and stimulate new accounts/new use of services within the strategy just noted.

Banking behavior was addressed in this study--current types of accounts, actual use of banking services, knowledge-ability of financial matters, frequency of use, customer's own criteria for bank selection, and their requirement regarding the important delivery system. Attitudes toward banking and toward other financial instituions were established, as well; using an attribute list determined through small scale studies rather than pre-selected, reaction to problem areas and a projective device involving attitudes attributed to others regarding their use of bank services. Plus, a battery of questions involving new service features, new modes of service and the rating of competitive banks relative to Chase. Demographics too, of course, entered into the questionnaire. The analysis interrelated demographic factors, behavioral factors, those of an attitudinal nature and the relative profitability of various mixes of bank services for a sample of 1,118 customers and non-customers.

Although not all attitudinal studies do help segment the market, this analysis showed that the market could be divided into discrete attitudinal segments based upon groups of decision makers who held similar views, had similar wants and needs relative to banking services yet different from other groups. A hypothetical example; cost concerned, investment oriented, credit favorable, personal service emphasis, etc.

The tactical program which is evolving from these data include a number of next steps.

1. Identify the profitability of these attitudinal segments in real terms related to the actual banking services used plus estimates of their likely actions to judge future value, e.g., cross-selling, repeat loans, multiple services.

2. Determine the demographic make-up of the more potentially profitable segments. Determine from area block data as closely as feasible the location and concentration of those potentially more profitable segments. Package banking services to be most attractive to satisfy customer needs. Possibly locating new branches, or mini branches, may be an outcome of this portion of the program.

3. Communicate the program internally--to product management, to operational areas (training)--and that is an important and no simple task.

4. Determine test and measurement criteria, develop advertising, point of sale promotions and direct mail support that emphasize the desires of the targeted segments.

Attitudinal research is one of many methods in use today as a means of gathering useful information to help define areas of competition differentiation, to help reinforce product and service relationships and to focus on resource allocation for profitability. I feel we are beginning to use it more effectively as a measurement method in banking. And as a relative newcomer to attitudinal research, we can and will, take full advantage of the considerable work done by others in this area before us. From the many fine speeches given during this conference, I know I've received nourishment for new thinking, new approaches, even some new applications and limitations.

Ladies and gentlemen, it's been my privilege to speak to this group today. Thank you for inviting me.

APPLICATIONS OF SURVEY RESEARCH IN CORPORATE DECISION-MAKING

Rene' D. Zentner, Shell Oil Company, Houston

ABSTRACT

As the business climate changes, there is an increasing need for decision-makers to improve their ability to follow such environmental shifts. Survey research is increasingly being employed both to measure external and internal changes, and to improve corporate decisions about responding to such changes.

INTRODUCTION

In recent years the environment of American business has become increasingly hostile. It is by now trite to observe that public trust in American business has declined; the Yankelovich, Skelly & White series on the dramatic drop in that confidence over the last ten years is well-known. Those data reveal that in 1979 only about a fifth of the American public believed business tries to strike a fair balance between profits and the public interest, down from the 70% who held that belief in 1968 (1979).

This decline in public confidence has been accompanied by dramatic changes in American society. It is not the purpose of this paper to examine those changes, except to say that they were associated with such major social events as the Viet Nam War and its termination, the Watergate scandal and the resignation and pardoning of President Nixon, the 1973/1974 Arab oil embargo, and the current turmoil in the Middle East.

Responding to these changes has been the formation in American society of organized political action groups having one or more limited purposes. These groups include those of consumers intending to affect corporate market behavior, of environmentalists intending to affect corporate disposal of gaseous, liquid and solid wastes, and of interested citizens intending to affect the production and consumption of energy-saving fuels. In most instances, the activities of these groups and the responses of state and national legislatures directly affected not only the manner in which corporate decisions were made, but also the nature of the decisions themselves.

Historically, people in corporations have made decisions on the basis of information coming from within the corporation itself. Research departments generated scientific information; engineering departments provided technical information, financial departments reported financial information, manufacturing departments generated production information, and marketing departments gave sales information, all about the conduct and performance of the corporation. That such information has in the past been sufficient is evidenced by the success of the American system of corporate management.

However, as American society changed, this type of information became insufficient. Traditional types of business information failed to provide insights into all of the social sectors in which the business enterprise was involved, including: changing attitudes of workers and managers toward work, changing attitudes of consumers toward product prices and quality, changing attitudes of factory neighbors toward noise and emissions, and changing attitudes by legislators about regulating business. In order to keep business decisions relevant, it became necessary for business executives to consider in their making of decisions information on the attitudes, behavior and intentions of the public in general and many of its particular parts.

In this paper, I will address several of the ways in which survey research has been employed to improve the quality of business decisions. In particular, I will discuss how data from survey research are developed, how companies are organized to acquire such data, and how such data are applied to decisions.

DEVELOPMENT OF RESEARCH INFORMATION

By "survey research", the writer intends to mean the development of information by asking selected respondents questions in some organized fashion, and recording and analyzing their responses. Under this general heading are grouped such specialized uses as market research and public opinion polling.

A variety of techniques are employed for the conduct of survey research. These methods include personal interviews, telephone interviews, mail questionnaires, and purchase or behavior diaries. Topics examined by these methods may address past behavior, such as brands of gasoline or soap purchased in the last month, present attitudes, such as current views on President Carter, national energy policy or toothpaste brands, or future intentions, such as vacation plans, automobile or

186

refrigerator purchases, or choices of potential Presidential candidates.

Data of these types can be obtained in a number of ways. A number of major U.S. research firms periodically collect public attitudes on current social and political issues. The information resulting from such measurements can be purchased on a subscription basis. Exemplary firms affording such services include Yankelovich, Skelly & White, Inc., Louis Harris & Associates, Inc., Cambridge Reports, Inc., Opinion Research Corporation, and The Roper Organization, Inc. In general, the topics studied and the questions used are determined by the survey firm itself, though frequently with the guidance of its clients. The frequency of the reports varies, from two studies each month in ORC's Public Opinion Index, to the annual survey reported in Yankelovich, Skelly & White's Corporate Priorities.

For many users of survey research, however, the information provided by the syndicated studies alone is not sufficient. The studies may not explore some issues with the thoroughness required by the individual user, or the questions of interest may not be repeated frequently enough in any particular year. As a result, a number of companies supplement the syndicated studies to which they subscribe with their own proprietary tracking surveys.

Such proprietary studies have a number of advantages over the multi-client syndicated studies. First, the content of the questionnaire is entirely under the control of the user. Thus, the user can determine the frequency with which any particular issue is explored during each year. Equally important is that the results of the survey can be kept confidential by the user, rather than share them with other sponsors as in the case of syndicated studies. For this reason, proprietary tracking studies are used to follow such sensitive issues as advertising effectiveness, competitor performance, and product acceptance. Moreover, the proprietary survey can be conducted as frequently as the client elects: weekly, monthly, quarterly, or annually as information needs dictate.

In addition to these syndicated or proprietary tracking studies, data are generally obtained through particular studies conducted on problems which arise from time to time. These studies can be carried out to obtain more detailed information than is provided by the tracking studies, or to obtain extensive data on a specific issue of interest.

Methods for conducting these tracking or project studies are extensively discussed in the literature, and will not be dealt in this article.

ORGANIZATION FOR SURVEY RESEARCH

Survey research for political purposes began in the middle 1930's as the result of work conducted at Princeton University. By the 1960's, public opinion polling on the major issues of the day had become an established feature of the national political process.

This lesson was not lost on the marketing profession. Professor Theodore Levitt of Harvard University has pointed out that George Gallup's work in opinion polling showed that there was a respectably scientific way of finding out what people really believed and wanted (Advertising Age 1976). Market research as the direct descendant of political opinion research quantified, qualified and developed the idea of market segmentation into a directly measurable and usable organizing principle. In the last three decades, marketing research has matured into a well established and accepted discipline with a literature, learned societies, and an extensive array of practitioners.

As a result, most of the survey research conducted by American industry is devoted to marketing research. In a 1969 study, The Role and Organization of Marketing Research, (Forman and Bailey 1969), the types of marketing research activities identified were research on markets, research on sales, research on products, research on advertising and promotion, and research on corporate growth and development.

In a survey of 237 manufacturing and non-manufacturing companies, the Conference Board found that more than 90% of both types of companies engage in each category of research.

The same study described the several organizational ways in which marketing research is conducted by the companies examined. While over 90% of the participants in the survey had marketing research departments of their own, many relied as well on outside help: specialized marketing research firms, consultants, and advertising agencies. For the companies reporting in the 1969 study, consumer products companies spent about 45% of their research budget on outside help, and industrial or non-manufacturing companies spent only about 10%.

While most of corporate opinion survey effort is devoted to marketing research, an increasing amount is being addressed

188

to other aspects of public opinion. There is a growing interest in the social and political changes in the corporate environment. When the Conference Board recently examined current
and future critical issues viewed by corporate officers, business credibility and government overregulation headed the
list. Thus, the corporations' customers are not the only important factor of the corporate environment; other publics are
also important. How these publics are ranked was revealed by
the Conference Board study. Heading the list was the federal
government, followed by customers and the financial community.

Understanding the changing nature of the corporate environment requires a variety of methods. These include monitoring the media and the literature for important signals of
change. But much of environmental research is public opinion
research. It is through the following of public attitudes that
one can follow and perhaps anticipate changes in the corporations' social and political environment.

In many companies, survey research operations are divided
between marketing research functions and public affairs organizations. Thus, research for support of the products'organizations is carried out by those organizations themselves. Research for examination of the social and political environment
is carried out in the public affairs or corporate planning
organizations. Typical of such divisions is that at companies
as disparate as Procter & Gamble, General Electric, and Exxon
Corporation. In others, all survey research is conducted by a
single research group which carries out market research, public
opinion polling, and advertising research studies. Shell Oil
Company has such a central group.

APPLICATION OF SURVEY RESEARCH TO CORPORATE DECISION-MAKING

Mr. Humphrey Taylor of Louis Harris & Associations, Inc.
has recently pointed out that companies use the information
provided by survey research in literally hundreds of different
ways. He has divided those ways into those used to make
internal changes affecting their procedures, policies, products
or services, and those employed to influence the external environment through communication aimed at the public, at opinion
leaders, legislators in Washington and state capitols, or at
those who influence leadership opinion. Sometimes, of course,
the research influences both internal and external activities.

It is trite to point out that survey research, whatever
the area and topic studied, should be such that the client can
employ its result in deciding upon a course of action to be

taken or not taken. In this section, we will examine some of the principal areas for such action.

With respect to marketing, the literature describing the techniques and application of survey research to the marketing of goods and services is extensive. No useful purpose would be served in either reciting that literature or in adding to it. Marketing research is the principal activity of the survey research organization, both corporate and independent, and most of those involved in research are aware both of how marketing research is conducted and how its results are employed in marketing decisions.

Advertising research presents a somewhat more provocative situation. Historically, most advertising has been an important part of the corporate marketing effort, designed to support the merchandising of goods and services. In such endeavors, advertising research played a key role, assisting the advertiser to evaluate the effectiveness of his advertising executions, and media choices. Like marketing research, such advertising research has been well documented.

In recent years, however, an increasing proportion of corporate advertising expenditures have been devoted to corporate advertising, advertising which does not support a product or service of the corporation. Instead, its purpose is to stress the corporation itself, its range of benefits to the nation at large, or its views on social or political issues.

That effort put into corporate advertising has risen sharply in the last five years is evidenced by a recent survey conducted by the Association of National Advertisers. Their survey of over three hundred major U.S. corporations showed that between 1975 and 1980, expenditures for corporate advertising increased 38%. The main objective of that advertising was to improve "the level of awareness of the company." Reported as including provision for corporate advertising in their advertising budgets were diversified corporations (85%), large diversified industrial marketers, and petroleum companies (88%) (Adweek 1979). The rise in corporate advertising has continued. In the ANA survey, 58% of the respondents have increased corporate advertising expenditures over the last three years.

For example, in recent color magazine advertisements, the French manufacturer Renault has been describing its entry into associations with U.S. companies. The insurance industry has played an active role in corporate advertising. The Hartford Insurance Group has described in current magazines its effectiveness in reducing truck hijacking.

Needs of the consumer have been addressed as well. Both General Motors and Shell Oil Company advertisements show methods to improve automobile maintenance and increase fuel efficiency. Many banks are currently supporting advertisements showing how to use bank facilities more efficiently.

The activities to provide energy for the nation have been a favorite subject for U.S. oil and coal companies. Such companies as Exxon, Texaco, Tenneco, Cities Service, Conoco, and Chevron have all addressed various aspects of their contribution to natural energy supply.

Advocacy advertising intended to present a company viewpoint to the public is perhaps the most visible area of corporate advertising. As in the case of corporate advertising, there has recently been an increase in corporate interest in making its views known. The ANA study showed between 1977 and 1979, the number of companies listing as their primary objective "to inform, educate or advocate relative to public issues" increased from 12% to 16% (Adweek 1979).

One especially interesting point derived from survey research is the tone in which advocacy advertising is to be couched. Advocacy advertisements supporting industry forest management practices, supported for some years by the American Forest Institute, were found to be quite effective. Fifty per cent of the government leaders surveyed and 70% of the public thought they were useful in supplying them with information on forestry issues. Advertising testing revealed that the more argumentative the advertising was, the less convincing it became. Accordingly, AFI's current advocacy campaign is a low key explanation and endorsement of forest management and conservation (Marketing and Media Decisions 1979). In testing the advertisements with respondents from Washington as well as from forest product plant communities, AFI found that extreme positions were not as effective as more moderate positions.

These strategies are new, as are the social issues that have provoked them. Each advertising campaign by each sponsor has a different objective, intended to enhance the sponsor's reputation, support the sponsor's causes or constituencies, or persuade the sponsor's audience. Advertising research plays a crucial role in the development, media selection and evaluation of such advertising. In some cases, evaluation of the lack of effectiveness of corporate advertising by other companies has caused a corporate sponsor to decide not to embark on a particular type of campaign.

191

CONSTITUENCY EVALUATION

As the intensity of social issues increases in the corporate environment, so the corporation becomes more concerned
about the attitudes of its constituencies and how to address
them. While those constituencies include the public and its
many components, constituencies closer to home cannot be overlooked. Thus, in recent years, companies have been surveying
attitudes of employees, retirees, shareholders, and the neighbors of their business and manufacturing operations.

Employee surveys are, of course, far from new. Over the
years, employee populations have been surveyed to determine
their attitudes about working conditions, employee benefits,
and other aspects of the working environment. As social and
political pressures on the corporation have grown, however,
employees are beginning to be perceived as a political consti-
tuency of growing importance.

At the same time, however, there are indications that employee alienation is on the increase. Studies have been conducted by Opinion Research Corporation over a period of the
last twenty-five years on employee attitudes and dissatisfaction.
Such data confirm that not only are employee values changing,
but that employee dissatisfaction is increasing, a problem with
which management must deal in the coming decade (Cooper et al.
1979). As such problems as these are recognized, management is
not only responding with policy changes but is developing messages to be communicated to employee constituencies through such
channels as mail, employee publications and local television
stations and newspapers. Survey research plays a key role in
the creation of such messages and in the evaluation of their
effectiveness. Thus, for many years the Bell System companies
have employed survey methods to determine the efficiency with
which employee publications carry their messages (Tirone 1977).

Social performance is also an issue of growing importance,
both inside and outside the company. Companies are not only
establishing social performance goals and programs but also em-
ploying survey research to determine how such programs are
working.

Exemplary of the measurement of progress in social issues
is that of Celanese Corporation. To monitor its practices in
that regard, it established in 1972 a Public Responsibility Committee,
comprising the five outside members of its Board of
Directors (Public Relations News 1979). Their purpose is to examine the
Company's activities and to oversee its practices in the pursuit of its
public responsibility goals. To secure data other than that afforded

192

through company channels, the Committee has independent authority to hire outside public opinion researchers to conduct surveys of the company's social performance. On the Committee's agenda during the Spring of 1979 were such issues as equal employment opportunity, the environment, employee safety, health and job satisfaction, product safety, energy conservation, and support of educational, cultural and health institutions.

Industrial companies are coming to recognize that one of their most important constituencies is made up of residents of the communities in which they do business. Many of those residents depend for their livelihood on supplying the company's plants, or the needs of the employees of those plants. Moreover, the plants are frequently major taxpayers in such communities, and play an important role in the social and economic life of the community. For these reasons, it is important that the company and the community are closely linked in their goals and activities, and that communications in both directions stay open and direct.

In understanding the nature of community attitudes, and in monitoring the effectiveness of Company communications, survey research has proved an important tool. For example, Shell Oil Company has for many years operated a major refinery and chemical plant in Norco, Louisiana; the Shell operation is the principal manufacturing enterprise in the community. As a consequence, it has endeavored to meet its responsibilities through various civic activities, and has communicated with Norco residents through newsletters, mail and the local newspaper. In the summer of 1978, Shell conducted a survey of Norco residents to determine how effectively it was seen as meeting those civic responsibilities. Also studied was whether its communications policy was working well. Results so obtained were employed in decisions affecting both the Company's civic activities and its communications program.

Shareholders have also been perceived as a group having the Company's interests at heart and as being in a position to take political action about those interests. Many companies are currently addressing their shareholders through annual reports, shareholder meetings, letters and other types of communications to take action at the state or federal level on issues important to the Corporation.

In order to evaluate the efficacy of such a communications program, the Public Service Company of Colorado mailed a questionnaire to its shareholders with its First Quarter 1978 report. To that inquiry, over a third of the shareholders replied, answering questions about Company policies and actions.

For example, 82% of the respondents agreed that Public Service should strongly oppose regulatory and legislative policies with which it disagreed. On the basis of the data received from the survey, the Company has continued policies supported by the shareholders, and is in the process of revising investor communications to include more regulatory and legislative information.

One of the most sophisticated systems for following public attitudes about a particular company is that which has been conducted since 1965 by the Corporate Public Relations Operation of General Electric Co. (Public Relations News 1979). Through the Westport firm of Trendex, Inc., General Electric carries out quarterly comprehensive surveys of 2000 adults and 1000 college students. While the study follows changes in public attitudes on national issues of interest to General Electric Co., it also evaluates the impact of the Company's corporate advertising programs, and affords an estimate of prospective demand for electricity.

Data from the survey are distributed to top General Electric executives, from Directors down through General Managers; recipients are spread across General Electric Company's 150 U.S. plant locations. In general, the information helps GE executives by creating awareness of changes in public attitudes toward particular issues, and how these issues affect General Electric. For example, the survey discovered steeply rising public opposition, which would kill approval by the U.S. Congress, of development of a U.S. supersonic transport, the contract for whose engines was held by General Electric. Other topics on which the General Electric system has collected data for at least a decade include fear of neighborhood crime, attitudes toward development of electric-powered automobiles, as well as willingness of Americans to approve spending for various types of environmental improvement.

Mr. Humphrey Taylor has perceptively pointed out that survey research confers its most important benefits to corporations in a subtle manner and one not discussed in the business literature. It does so by bringing a sense of reality into management offices and boardrooms. Mr. Taylor points out that a majority of senior executives are, almost inevitably, quite out of touch with the opinions, prejudices, criticisms, needs and values of much of the general public. Because they are usually surrounded throughout the working day by people who generally reinforce their own perceptions of what is going on in the outside world, and who fail to alert them to very real public pressures, their decisions are based on incomplete information. Mr. Taylor suggests that survey research can make an important contribution to corporate decision-making at a

194

time when more issues than ever before require the attention of corporate management, and at a time when issues seem to be more volatile and more complex than they were in preceding periods.

CONCLUSIONS

From the foregoing discussion, some general conclusions can be drawn. First, it is evident that the American business enterprise is becoming the focus of greater public attention than in the past. This attention takes the form of public concern and, occasionally, dissatisfaction with the Corporation's social behavior, its products and its treatment of its employees and its customers. Such concern is inevitably becoming the subject of public policy debate and, as a consequence, legislation and regulation affecting business behavior.

Companies have historically employed survey research for determining consumer preferences and to support marketing operations. But as social and political pressures on the business sector increase, survey research is moving out of the marketing department and into other areas. It is increasingly becoming a corporate tool for evaluating public attitudes toward company behavior, not only in the market but in society as a whole. As the foregoing illustrations reveal, survey research is answering questions about social acceptance of the corporate enterprise and its products that transcend the traditional markets. It can be expected that survey research will increasingly become employed by such corporate functions as public and governmental affairs groups as well as those charged with monitoring social performance and responsibility.

REFERENCES

Yankelovich, Skelly & White, Inc. (1979), Corporate Priorities 1979, New York.

Advertising Age (1976), April 12.

Forman, Lewis W. and Earl L. Bailey (1969), The Role and Organization of Marketing Research, Experiences in Marketing Management, The Conference Board, New York: No. 20.

McGrath, Phyllis S. (1976), Managing Corporate External Relations, New York: A Research Report from The Conference Board's Division of Management Research.

Adweek/Southwest Advertising News (1979), (November 5), p. 38.

Adweek/Southwest Advertising News, loc. cit.

Marketing and Media Decisions (1979), (June), p. 64.

Cooper, M. R., B. S. Morgan, P. M. Foley, and L. B. Kaplan (1979), "Changing Employee Values: Deepening Discontent?" Harvard Business Review (January-February), 117-125.

Tirone, James F. (1977), "Measuring the Bell System's Public Relations," Public Relations Review, Winter, 21-38.

Public Relations NEWS (1979), XXXV, (May 7), Number 19.

Public Relations News, loc. cit.